volume 5 Practical Helps from Godl

the complete guide to

Godly Play

iwonder

An imaginative method for presenting scripture stories to children edited by Dina Strong

ISBN 1-931960-04-6

TABLE OF CONTENTS

FOREWORD

BY JEROME W. BERRYMAN

The authors of this volume are nearly all accredited Godly Play trainers. It has been written not only to introduce you to some of the next generation of leaders in Godly Play, but also to make available to you the benefit of their experience and insight. In addition to about one-third of our trainers being represented here you will also meet the Director of Theological Inquiry for the Center for the Theology of Childhood, Dr. Marcia Bunge, and our Director for Empirical Research, Dr. Rebecca Nye, who is also one of two accredited Godly Play Trainers in the United Kingdom.

The kind of help you will find here for your continuing development as a Godly Play teacher supplements the first four volumes of *The Complete Guide to Godly Play* and their related videos. You will find here wisdom about developing the storyteller you already are. There is advice about how to manage time and space in the classical teaching and learning environment for Godly Play and for working with Godly Play "outside the box" of that environment. In addition, there is commentary about how to nourish relationships in the community of children, wherever you find them, and with adults involved in Godly Play. Since there is nothing quite so practical as good theory there are also reflections about children's education, their spirituality and a theology of childhood for adults, based on what has been learned about children in Godly Play settings around the world so we adults can be guided toward entering the reality Jesus called "the Kingdom of Heaven."

Who are these Godly Play trainers? I wish these pages could introduce you to all of them, but their time and this volume's space will not permit it. They come from a variety of backgrounds including distinguished academics, parish priests, military chaplains, stay-at-home moms and working moms, full-time teachers of children in public schools, leaders in the ministry of teaching in churches, etc. They also come from a wide spectrum of denominations: Anglicans, Presbyterians, Quakers, Methodists, Church of Christ (DOC), Pentecostals and others.

What accredited Godly Play trainers have in common is a love for the scriptures and the ability to invite children, God and adults to "come out and play" together to make meaning and to find ethical direction about life and death for all ages and stages of faith development. They are first of all Godly Play teachers with a deep respect for children. They also have the ability to learn from the children they teach in a kind of mutual blessing, which keeps improving them in this art of Godly Play. In short, they know how to play. In addition all have experienced a week long training process that enables them to guide the eighteen contact hour teacher accreditation training events. They are also prepared to design and lead a variety of other kinds of Godly Play introductions, consultations and training. In addition they must participate in continuing education to keep their accreditation and themselves fresh.

The source of Godly Play training, research, service, and writing is The Center for the Theology of Childhood in Houston, Texas, but it takes more than these kinds of activities to keep Godly Play clearly defined yet creative, supportive, growing and profoundly playful. It takes a whole triangle of different kinds of activity. Godly Play Resources in Ashland, Kansas is the second part of the triangle. This is where beautiful, long-lasting, well-tested and useful teaching objects are crafted and made available to you. The third part of this triangle of support comes from our publishers, especially Living the Good News in Denver, Colorado, where this series and their related videos have been published.

Godly Play is much more than "the latest thing" in Christian education. It is very old rather than new. This is because Godly Play is rooted in ancient storytelling and the educational theory and practice founded by Dr. Maria Montessori (1870-1952), which helps teach the children how to listen well to such storytelling and to be active in their learning and interpretations of the scriptures and worship for their lives. This is especially important in a time when children are being taught to be consumers of teaching, things and entertainment, which is sometimes confused with Christian education. Instead, we invite children to be active interpreters of what is of lasting importance in life and death. Most importantly, Godly Play draws together the scriptures, the experience of God, the worship traditions and reflections by Christians and our Jewish forbearers into a kind of playful orthodoxy.

May you find in these volumes what you need to enter into the most rewarding play of all: Godly Play.

CHAPTER 1
HELP WITH TELLING STORIES

THE GOOD SHEPHERD CALLED US

"Yea, tho I walk through the valley of the shadow of death, I will fear no evil, for Thou art with me..."

I think it should be noted that on the Sunday after September 11, 2001, I called all of our classes together and used the Parable of the Good Shepherd as a way to have conversation about the tragedy of the World Trade Center. I think it should be noted because, as I talked to trainers around the country later that week, it seems we all had done much the same thing. The Good Shepherd had called to us. And many of us had turned to Psalm 23 to read it to our children, a source of comfort in our lives, as it was in our parents and grandparents' lives and in the lives of all the grandparents before them. "The Lord is my shepherd, I shall not want..."

—Kim McPherson

THE STORIES SPEAK FOR THEMSELVES

by Jennifer Acland

The children gather eagerly. They have not heard these stories before.

I teach religious education in a non-denominational Christian school for girls in Melbourne, Australia. The school has Christianity woven into its foundation, but many of the families in the school would have only a very occasional church connection with it. Some parents have been married in the local churches, and they may well be buried from those churches when the time is right, but worship is not part of their life routine.

I wanted to know if religious education inspired by Godly Play would work in an Australian Primary school. I was appointed as the Junior School Chaplain after I ran an in-service training to introduce the teachers to Godly Play. The teachers welcomed the change in approach and me.

The children sit, silent and mesmerized by the movement, the material, the voice: the story. We journey together through the desert, we seek God's face and we long for the Temple. Later we listen to Jesus' words and wonder what his life and death might mean for us.

Listening to the silence as I told the stories, hearing their remarkable responses and seeing their beautiful artwork all made me think of ways to invite them deeper, through the stories, to the place where they might encounter God. I wanted to tell them more stories, more stories of individual people doing the very thing I was inviting them to do. I told them about Balaam and Gideon and Saul, the first King. I wanted to tell more stories of women who listened to God. So I wrote about Ruth and Naomi and Hannah. Later I told about the woman at the well and about Martha who worked and Mary who sat. I told them about the woman and her oil. They continued to wonder and to do their work.

I do not use many of the stories from the Liturgical Cycle as the children I teach do not go to church. Instead I stay close to the scripture stories as we have them. Staying true to the inspiration and practice of Godly Play I have written new stories. I am a member of the Australian Network of Biblical Storytellers. They encourage people to learn scripture passages for recitation in church rather than always hearing it read. I have found their method meshes beautifully with the reflective silence of Godly Play. Children who have not heard the stories come fresh to them. It is a delight to tell the stories and to watch them being received like bread from heaven.

I speak the words of scripture straight from the book, or so it seems to the listeners. I learn the passage from their *Good News Bibles* and I speak those words to them.

They have not heard words exactly like these before. And yet they echo with a distant familiarity.

"Do you know the whole Bible, Miss?"

I smile at their wonder. They find the story for themselves in the book and they hear the echo again. And again, I pray... The stories speak for themselves.

THE SLOW PACE OF GODLY PLAY

by Kathleen Capcara

When I travel to other Godly Play classrooms to lead workshops, I often hear teachers worry about the need to "slow down." Helping children learn the skill of being still to allow more openness to the presence of God is certainly a part of Godly Play. But I believe some of the urgency about telling stories slowly may come from a feeling of the need to emulate the style of Godly Play's founder, Jerome Berryman.

The Reverend Doctor Berryman is a gifted storyteller. His soft voice, slow delivery and gentle manner in presenting lessons have held us spellbound for years. But I believe that in modeling the Godly Play method for us, it was never his intention for every Godly Play storyteller to become exactly like him. All of us who present Godly Play lessons will need to find our own style and authentic voice. I also believe that it is often appropriate to modify your storytelling style to suit the ages of the children and specific situations in your classroom. A slightly faster pace may work better with older children and in some situations.

Some of the slower pace of Godly Play stories is necessitated by the use of manipulative story telling materials. It is difficult to tell a story quickly and move materials that illustrate the story at the same time. And learners find it challenging to simultaneously watch what you do with the materials while they listen to what you say as you present the lesson. The ability to process both verbal and visual information at the same time improves with age in many learners, but not all.

The children in your classrooms who are extroverts will be quick to let you know when they feel the pace of your storytelling is too slow. But try to remember that there will also be introverts in your class who may not verbalize their appreciation of the slower pace.

I live on the East coast, where a premium is placed on accomplishing things quickly. I believe that some of this comes from a desire to do as many good things as possible in the limited time we have on earth. As one of these well-intentioned people, I need to remind myself that when the prophet Elijah was waiting for God to come to him, Elijah was sitting still in a cave. And God was not in the earthquake, wind or fire that passed by Elijah. God came in a sound of sheer silence. It takes a slower pace to be fully present to a sound of sheer silence. I use a prayer by Michael Leunig to remind myself and my restless fourth and fifth graders to find the peace and serenity that are already in our hearts: "God help us to live slowly...to move simply...to look softly...to allow emptiness...to let the heart create for us."

GETTING READY TO TELL STORIES

by Becki Stewart

Practicing
- Your goal is to make the story your own.
- Choose a lesson you love or are familiar with.
- Begin by reading through the script.
- Use the lesson materials or substitutes so you learn the story with your body.
- Practice with cue cards. Highlight key words. As you practice without notes, use the cards when you forget.
- Audio tape yourself and listen to the story over and over.
- Practice in front of a mirror and watch the movements.
- Practice telling the story to a safe audience.

Developing Your Style
• Be patient with yourself, it takes time.
• You have your own unique style.
• The story belongs to all people and the children need to know that.
• Just do it.

Making "Mistakes"
• It happens.
• Just keep going.
• Make a choice—leave it or correct it when you can.
• Use your mistakes: learn from them.

STORIES FROM THE HEART: WHY IT'S IMPORTANT TO LEARN GODLY PLAY STORIES BY HEART

by Rosemary Beales

Sometime teachers are afraid they cannot memorize the stories, and that they need to rely on written prompts such as note cards to help them present the story to children. Here are the reasons that it's important to make the effort to work "without a net."

First, "learning stories by heart" is a more accurate description of what we do than the word "memorizing." I hope it will transform the process from a task that must be accomplished to a joy that may be embraced.

When a story sinks into your heart, it also comes from your heart in the telling. Children know the difference!

Learning the stories by heart:
• allows the story to take root in you so that it becomes your own and nourishes your own spirit
• removes the distraction of having to look in two different places—the text and the materials—as you present the story (Focusing your visual attention on the materials actually helps you remember the language.)
• gives the children only one place to look, at the story materials (This focuses their attention as well as yours.)
• shows children that you love the story so much that you know it by heart
• enables you, eventually, to become fluent enough that you can work with any child who chooses any story material at response time

The language of the Godly Play texts is carefully chosen, and it is important to be attentive to the language. But it is even more important to be relaxed and enter into the story you are presenting. Telling the story from your heart, to the children's hearts, is more important than getting it right.

THE LANGUAGE OF GODLY PLAY

by Becki Stewart

Jerome Berryman identifies four kinds of language in a Godly Play classroom.

The Language of Sacred Stories:
- described by Jerome Berryman as narratives in which God is the main character
- tells about the encounters of the people of God with the mystery of the presence of God
- helps us find our own story within the Master Story (the Bible)
- tells about finding our identity as children of God

The wondering questions for the Sacred Stories include:
- I wonder what part of the story you like best?
- I wonder what part of the story is most important?
- I wonder what part of the story is about you or where are you in the story?
- I wonder what part of the story we could leave out and still have all the story we need?

The Language of Parables:
- pushes language to the limit
- illustrates that the Kingdom of God is not something that can be expressed easily using ordinary language
- encourages us to make sense of life in existential terms (meaning, death, aloneness, freedom)
- stands on its own (You can't throw a parable away just because you have discovered one correct interpretation.)
- includes the "I Am" statements of Jesus
- speaks in the authentic voice of Jesus

The wondering questions for the Parables include:
- I wonder what this could really be?
- I wonder where this could really be?
- I wonder who the person could really be?
- I wonder if the birds have names? If they are happy? If they know how to build

their nests? I wonder what the person was doing while the seed was growing? I wonder if the person was happy to see the birds nest in the tree? If the person could take the shrub that grew as big as if it were a tree and put it back inside the tiny seed?

- I wonder how he felt now that he had the great pearl? I wonder why the seller would give up the great pearl? If the seller was happy with all his things? I wonder what could be so precious that a person would exchange everything for it? I wonder if the seller had a name? I wonder if you have ever come close to the great pearl?

The Language of Liturgy:
- means "the work of the people"
- shows how we as a community of Christians worship God
- demonstrates the parts of a particular Christian act, such as baptism
- shows how time and space are ordered for a community of Christians (i.e. How the Church Tells Time)
- shows the meaning of the act of worship through symbols and symbolic actions (i.e. The Mystery of Easter)

The wondering questions for the Liturgical lessons include:
- I wonder if you have seen something like this in church?
- I wonder what happens when you see the colors?
- I wonder what part of Lent you like the best?
- I wonder if you have come close to a table like this?

The Language of Silence:
- helps children become aware of the elusive presence of God
- enables children to be ready to hear the small, still voice
- supports the creative process and an ability to contemplate the lesson
- gives us the opportunity to experience silence and become comfortable with it

The wondering questions about silence may include:
- I wonder where the silence is?
- I wonder where the silence comes from?
- I wonder how the silence makes you feel?
- I wonder how the silence speaks to you?

The language of Godly Play gives children a way to confront the existential questions common to all people. The questions we all struggle with are about the meaning of life, death, freedom and aloneness.

The goal of Godly Play is helping children to learn to use religious language to know God and find direction in their lives while they are still young.

—Jerome Berryman

WHAT IS AN OBJECT BOX?

by Kathleen Capcara

Some Native American and African storytellers used a storytelling bag. Objects pulled from the bag would remind the storyteller of an important story. The listeners would feel a certain amount of suspense as they wondered what object would come out of the bag next and what story might be connected with the object.

Jerome Berryman suggests object boxes to hold symbols from some of the important stories of our tradition. Many of the Bible stories we use in the liturgy just tell one incident in the life of a character such as Abraham. An object box story can provide an in-depth look at the life of a character—a timeline of what happened to Abraham, for example. Object boxes can also tell the stories of saints, church leaders and spiritual leaders such as Ghandi or Martin Luther King Jr. Or the boxes can hold stories about church customs such as "What is a Bishop?" or "Traditions of Christmas."

Object boxes are especially appropriate for older children, ages 6-12. The small objects appeal to children in that age range and pose no danger to them.

Object boxes are designed for children to work with. As they examine and lay out the objects in the box, they learn how to tell the story that the objects represent. The objects need to be durable enough to withstand use by many small and large hands.

When telling a story using an object box, lay out the items in a line using a carpet square as a background. Place the items in order from your right to your left. As the children see the items, they will appear from left to right—the way we learn to read in English.

It is not a good idea to pass the items from the object box around the circle as you tell the story. It is too distracting for the children. Instead, remind them that they can work with the box later.

A control should be included with each object box—a length of poster board that contains a simple black drawing of each object and the order in which it appears when telling the story. This provides a means for the children to check their own work without help from an adult.

Often, after hearing object box stories, children are inspired to research and make their own object box. It can be a marvelous way to preserve the stories of our faith and life together for the next generation.

MAKING AN OBJECT BOX

by Kathleen Capcara

First, research the story. If it is a Bible story, read it in several translations and consult some commentaries. Discuss the story with your minister or spiritual director, Bible study group and/or Godly Play teachers' group. If it is a story about a saint or a person, read some biographies of the person. If it is a story about the Church's traditions, go to a church library, or ask your minister where you might find resources on the topic.

Second, write the story. Think about the important themes and shifts in action in the story. Write an outline of what you would like to say in the story, then write out the story. Let it sit for a day or two before you come back to it. Rewrite as necessary.

Third, decide what objects you will include in your story. Choose materials that help tell the story without being so interesting as to detract from it. When possible, use the highest quality materials you can afford to increase visual appeal for the children. Give preference to natural materials and durable materials that children can touch repeatedly. You can use small boxes within the object box itself to keep items organized and to add appeal.

Fourth, locate the objects. Some sources are craft stores, doll furniture stores, party goods (for trinkets and flags), discount department stores, Christmas ornament departments, toy stores, inexpensive import stores or catalogs and religious book stores. If you are unable to find or make what you need, consider using a photograph or drawing from a magazine, or from a church supply or publishing catalogue. You may need to give up on certain objects. You can still tell that part of the story without an object.

Fifth, test your story. You may be able to test the story on family members or friends, either adults or children. When you test your story in the classroom, listen to what children say. Watch their art responses. Keep the story in your room and observe the children. Do they come back to the story on their own?

Finally, offer your story to other teachers to test. Ask the teachers to report to you the reaction of the children to the story. Discuss any changes they would make and why.

CHAPTER 2
HELP WITH MANAGING TIME

A STORY LIKE YOURS

I was a door person in a classroom of children who did not know me well. The storyteller, who had known this group of children for a long time, had just presented the story of Jesus and the Twelve. Toward the end of the wondering, she asked, "I wonder which of the people in this story has a story like yours?" I expected children to talk about Jesus, perhaps, or about Peter.

But a girl in the circle replied, "Judas. My story is like Judas' because sometimes I betray my friends by telling their secrets." She thought a minute and added, "I need to work on trying not to do that."

Other children in the circle were quiet and beginning to squirm a bit, but the storyteller's only response was in a calm and neutral tone of voice: "Hmm." After a period of silence, she moved on to other questions, but I could see that an important transformation had happened in the circle of children that day. Trust was built because one girl had the courage to share a part of her story and the teacher helped make it safe to share by her non-judgmental response.

—Kathleen Capcara

WONDERING: OUR FIRST RESPONSE TO THE LESSON

by Kathleen Capcara

As a storyteller, one of the parts of leading Godly Play I like best is the first response from the circle of children after they hear the lesson. It's the part we call "wondering."

"I wonder." What a remarkable approach to what we have known for years as "Christian education." The phrase "I wonder" is so deeply at the core of Godly Play that it appears as a shadow in the right-hand margins of every page of these books. Wondering as a response to God's presence in the Bible stories and in our lives implies many things. The word "wonder" has so many layers of meaning that Webster's dictionary lists several separate definitions, and all of them apply to what we do in Godly Play.

The first definition of wonder, "the quality of exciting, amazed admiration," expresses our most immediate and natural response to Bible stories and religious traditions. As Godly Play storytellers, we use beautiful materials to present a lesson to the children. When the lesson is over, we sit back and look at the physical representation of the story present in the center of our circle. Words elude us as we sit marveling at God's work as it is revealed in the lesson—and now among us. All we can say at first is "wow!" But one of the goals of Godly Play is to help us learn religious language so we can use it together to find meaning in our experiences. Wondering is a way to move beyond the "wow" and into the second meaning of wonder: "to be curious or in doubt about."

Curiosity and doubt are not the first words most of us associate with the concept of education, not even religious education. For many years religious education has been about indoctrination and enculturation—passing on information about the teachings and traditions of our religious institution. As Christian educators, we have been trained to make sure the students have a firm grasp of the information we are handing over to them. The curiosity and doubt expressed by the phrase "I wonder" may not seem to have much to contribute to such serious business.

"I wonder what part of this story you like best?" the storyteller asks the children after the Godly Play lesson is presented. As I train Sunday school teachers who are working with children using the Godly Play method, the wondering after the lesson is one of the parts of Godly Play that makes them feel uneasy. "We often don't get much response from the children," they tell me. "How do we know they are getting it?" In fact, Godly Play teachers ask that first question in precisely those words to demonstrate to the children that we are not fishing for an answer here. We use the phrase "I wonder" to show the children we are curious about how they are thinking about the lesson and to remind them it is safe to share those thoughts with us. The use of "I wonder" makes the question an indirect one, which is our first clue to the children that our aim is not to put them on the spot. The second clue is in our words, "I wonder what *you* like best." Each individual listener will have a unique answer to that question because the question is about them and their specific response.

But why ask such a seemingly superficial question when we have so much important information about God and scripture and our religious traditions to teach the children? We ask wondering questions because keeping the questions open is the best way to invite people into a lifelong engagement with God and scripture and religious traditions.

When we ask a pointed question, like "What does the mustard seed represent in this story?" it most often has the effect of shutting the children down. They are not sure what the teacher is looking for. They become afraid of giving the "wrong answer" and appearing foolish. They feel frustrated because they have a sense that the teacher is fishing for something specific, and they are not sure what it is. They want to please the teacher by giving "the right answer," but they instinctively know that a lot of what religion is about is mystery. Children in this situation feel a double bind.

The whole point of Godly Play, of listening to the lessons and using them to find meaning in our experience, is to encourage more Godly Play. This is because as human beings we are on a lifelong search for meaning. We need to tell and retell the lessons, not learn them once and discard them because we think we have understood the essential information contained in the lesson. We think and wonder about the lessons to invite more thinking and wondering about the lessons—all week long, even after the teachers and the children have gone home.

What we teach in Godly Play is a way of living in wonder, in "rapt attention or astonishment at something mysterious or new to one's experience," a third definition from Webster. In the Episcopal Church, at baptism, we pray that the person being baptized will have "an inquiring and discerning heart, the courage to will and to persevere, a spirit to know and to love" and "the gift of joy and wonder" in all God's works. This is not a prayer evoking traditional Christian education. This is not a prayer about wanting the baptized to learn information. This is a prayer about living in wonder. It reminds us that as people who encounter God, our experiences are always changing, and we are constantly looking for the meaning of our lives. We have to keep the questions open so we and the children can be open to all the new ways God is acting around and in us.

A fourth definition of wonder listed in Webster's Dictionary is "effective or efficient beyond anything previously known or anticipated." The Godly Play approach is truly a wonder. The way we use wondering questions to encourage the children to reflect on the lesson is effective in ways unanticipated by all of us. Yes, often as we wonder with the children, we don't always immediately hear a verbal response. But posing open-ended questions after the lesson is just the beginning. Any discussion we engage in with the children as we sit in the circle is just the beginning of wondering.

Some of the children's answers to the wondering questions appear during the individual response time. Those wonderings by the children are nonverbal. Expressions of what the children are "wondering" appear as some children use art materials to make something that shows how they feel about the lesson, or as other children work with the storytelling materials to retell the lesson. Even these visible responses, however, are just the beginning of their wondering.

Once, when I was telling my third grade Godly Play class the story of "The Ten Best Ways to Live," I got no response from Susan when I asked the circle of children, "I wonder which of the ten best ways to live is hardest for you?" But Susan's mother telephoned me on Wednesday to tell me that when she was in the car riding home from school that day, Susan asked her mother the same question: "Mom, I wonder which of the ten best ways to live is hardest for you?" Susan's mother was astonished to think that as an adult, she had never been asked that question about the Ten

Commandments. The whole family talked about it at dinner that night. Now, that religious education was "effective or efficient beyond anything previously known or anticipated." Godly Play is a wonder.

THE ART OF MANAGING THE CIRCLE

by Becki Stewart

GETTING READY

- Make the story your own.
- Ready yourself on the inside; be calm, confident, patient with the process and trust God.
- Prepare the lesson materials and the room. The environment is an unspoken lesson.
- Be clear about your role and duties in the Godly Play room. Communicate with the other teacher.
- *Model* how to enter the language.
- *Show* your love for the language.
- *Respect* the power of the language, the presence of God and the relationship of the child with the Holy One.

MAKING THE CIRCLE

- Begin at the threshold. Help children get ready *before* they enter the room.
- Greet and seat each child individually.
- Help the children make a circle. "Let's make our circle big enough so everyone can see." "Would you be the anchor today?" "Do you remember how to get ready?"
- Model the ready position: legs folded and hands on the lap or on the knees.
- Check to see if the whole circle is ready.

SETTING THE TONE WITH RITUAL

- Give an informal greeting and visit with the children as the children enter.
- Greet one another formally: "The Lord be with you. And also with you."
- Change the calendar and recall where you are in the church year.

KEEPING CONTROL DURING THE LESSON

- Check your own attitude—calm, confident.
- Make sure each child and the door person are ready. Check the circle as a whole.
- Have clear expectations of behavior, consequences and procedures.
- Know the children and the lesson.
- Establish and maintain boundaries. Use language that is appropriate and respectful

to the children. "Be ready." "Only you can get yourself ready." "Walk around his space." "What lessons are you telling in the desert box?" "When I tell the lesson, I move the pieces. Later this can be your work."

- Find and develop your own voice and style. Be patient with yourself.
- Show children the act of making meaning by modeling the process.
- Invite children to enter the language. Don't erect barriers that prevent children from experiencing the presence of God.
- Model how you find your own meaning: "I hadn't thought of that." "I wonder about that too." "Hmm."
- Show how you value this language, time and space.
- Remember, the story's meaning is deeply personal. It is not given by the teachers, but is discovered by each individual.

HANDLING DISRUPTIONS

- Consider the individual. Look for motive and consider the circumstances.
- Provide boundaries, but realize some children will test these limits. Work hard to provide a *safe* place to explore and discover faith and meaning.
- Jerome Berryman offers a five-step sequence for handling disruptions. (See pages 69-70 in *The Complete Guide to Godly Play: Volume 1*.) Briefly summarized they are:
  1. Check your own involvement. Ignore the "small stuff."
  2. Look up briefly. Pause and break from the story briefly. Address the whole group, "We need to get ready again." Emphasize expected behavior. Hope that the child enters into the community by getting ready again.
  3. Specifically direct comments to the child, "No, that's not fair. Look at all the other children. You need to be ready too." Use a neutral tone of voice.
  4. Ask the child to get up and go sit by the door person. "*(Child's name),* please get up now and go find a place near the door person where you can still hear the story."
  5. Tell the child, "It is time to go now. May I help you or can you go by yourself?" Although it is preferred that the child choose to go to the door person, if necessary, gently but firmly carry the child to the door person.
- Teachers are in control of this time. Boundaries apply to the work time as they do during the lesson. Make this time as orderly as possible, using a routine and organized environment.

INVITING CHILDREN INTO RESPONSE TIME

- Dismiss children one at a time to do their work.
- Children may want to hear the story again or wish to work with another lesson. They may choose a different story only if they have heard it before. Encourage them to ask someone else to tell them the story. They may also choose to "work on themselves" or take care of things in the room. Both choices are important and appropriate work.

- The door person assists the child *if needed* to find, gather and use materials appropriately.
- Some days you may not have adequate time for work and you may decide to go directly to the feast from the lesson. If so, schedule a work day in the coming weeks when no lesson is presented and children can move quickly into choosing their work.
- The storyteller calls the children back to the circle for the feast. "It is time to put away your work. We have plenty of time, but you need to stop now and clean up your place. When you have done that, please come to the circle for the feast."
- Children replace all materials in their proper place. "We need to make the materials ready for the next person to use."

SHARING A FEAST TIME

- The door person chooses feast helpers.
- The storyteller centers the circle, encouraging children as they finish cleaning up.
- When the feast is served, bless the feast. Invite each child to pray, but allow children the right to pass.
- Sharing the feast provides a great opportunity to visit with the children.
- Have each child clean up his or her place.

MANAGING CLOSURE

- The door person watches for parents to arrive and calls each child (one at a time) to say goodbye to the storyteller.
- The storyteller offers hands to each child and gives each a blessing. This time is critical to building a trusting relationship with the child. Support and value that child each and every time you are together.

FINISHING THE DAY

- If possible, silently reflect upon the time spent with the children.
- Talk with the other teacher about the class that day.
- Clean and straighten the room for the next Godly Play class.

TIPS ABOUT WONDERING TOGETHER

by Kathleen Capcara

As the Godly Play lesson is presented, most storytellers keep their gaze focused on the materials. As the wondering begins, looking up and around at the circle of children is a good way to indicate that you welcome verbal responses from them after a period of listening to you talk.

Children who are introverted may feel "put on the spot" if you make direct eye contact with them as you pose a wondering question. For this reason, after asking each wondering question, some storytellers look back down at the lesson materials in front of them as they wait for the children to respond.

A period of silence after a question is presented sometimes makes the storyteller feel alone, as if no one has heard the question or no one understood the story. Silence can be difficult for many people, especially extroverts, but silence is an important part of wondering. Just as the storyteller sits in silence before beginning the lesson to allow it to form inside of him or her, the circle of children needs silence to allow the wondering to form within them.

If you have difficulty allowing for silence, try looking at the materials and silently, within your own mind, answering the wondering question you just asked. The time you take to wonder for yourself allows the children some time to wonder.

If there is still only silence from the circle of children, remember it does not mean your presentation of the lesson was ineffective. Avoid the temptation to direct a wondering question to a specific child. It is really not good to say, "Ryan, I wonder what part of the story *you* like best?" There is no reason to expect each child to respond to the lesson on someone else's timetable. It will happen in God's time.

There are many reasons that children don't immediately talk out loud about the Godly Play lesson:

- They don't have the words to express how the lesson affects them—yet they feel the effect of God's presence as the lesson is presented, and it leaves them speechless.
- They have introverted personalities or learning styles that don't favor giving an immediate verbal response to new information and ideas. Researchers tell us that people who learn best by hearing process more slowly than visual learners, and people who process information through movement respond to new information even more slowly than those with the other two styles.
- They are afraid of giving the wrong answer and feeling foolish. This fear will diminish over time as the storyteller and circle of children build trust as they wonder together. It is important for the storyteller to indicate the value in each child's contribution to the wondering. A good way to do this is with a thoughtful nod of the head and a neutral verbal sound like "hmm."

When a child responds to a wondering question in a way that seems unrelated to the lesson, some storytellers point to the materials as a way of refocusing the child as they say, "That is very interesting, but right now we are trying to think and talk about this lesson." If the child is excited to share an unrelated story, remind him or her that, "We can talk about that during the feast."

If your circle of children has one or more extroverts who tend to dominate the wondering, and you sense that others really want to speak, you can say, "I wonder if anyone else has a part of the story they like best."

Remember that the purpose of wondering is not to reassure the storyteller that she was effective in presenting the lesson. Nor is it to get the children to summarize the lesson so they leave with a single "take home message" or "Reader's Digest" condensed version to share with parents. The purpose of wondering is to invite the children to think about the lesson all week long. Trust that the Holy Spirit will work in the children long after they have left the classroom.

ON DIALOGUE AND GODLY PLAY

by Kim McPherson

Years after I had begun Godly Play in my church, I learned about the practice of dialogue. It was a word I'd tossed around for years, but one that I came to find I had not fully understood. I'm beginning to suspect that about Godly Play, too—that what I talked about in my earlier years is not the Godly Play I've come to know. The good news is that my understanding continues to grow, and my definitions continue to be enriched. This isn't an "add water and mix" curriculum. This is the stuff that journeys are made of; it requires kneading like bread for the journey of life, and my deep conviction—one that I learned from Jerome Berryman's example—is that we need only the confidence to begin. Like putting our hands in a bowlful of bread dough, ragged, dry and with so much flour it seems we could never mix it in, if we keep on kneading, we will gain understanding, improve our dialogue, learn to appreciate the quality of silence, and find the right questions. Eventually, we make bread.

In *CommunityWorks 2002*, Debbie Asberry writes:

> Dialogue is a way of being in conversation that invites our own deepest self-open-ing and knowing and creates the space for the collective wisdom to emerge. It is a discipline that requires openness, emptiness, mystery and beginner's mind. It is about inquiry, listening, compassion, courage and delight. Informed by our silence and authentic conversations, we increase our capacity for creativity and right action.

According to Asberry, dialogue looks like this:
- Sit in a circle.
- Stop talking. Take a vow of silence. Speak only to improve on the silence and to be in service of meaning and community.
- Openness is the rule, not the exception.
- Listen to understand.
- Pay attention to your intentions.

- Notice your assumptions and inner voice.
- Imagine the other person's perspective.
- Explore the other's intentions, assumptions, through inquiry. "Do you mean...?" "What is your understanding of...?"
- Allow others to see your perspective and your assumptions.
- Question from a place of genuine "not-knowing."
- See the divine in others: *Seek and serve Christ in others.*
- Stop talking. Take a vow of silence. Speak only to improve on the silence and to be in service of meaning and community.

Once Jerome Berryman suggested to me that when a child in the circle is being disruptive (in the way we all recognize, that takes attention away from the story and the storyteller), I could say, *"I wonder what you really mean?"* or *"I wonder what you are really trying to tell me?"*

I had occasion to use that advice soon after, with good result. I was telling the parable of the mustard seed, when a little boy in the circle began acting out. His movements were distracting and he began firing comments that didn't have anything to do with the story. (Sound familiar?) So I looked at him and asked the question: *"I wonder what you are really trying to tell me?"* That quieted him, and I went back to the story. I put the birds into their nests in the trees, telling how the mustard plant had become a large bush, large enough that the birds could build their nests in its branches, when this child blurted out: "My parents are getting a divorce and I don't know where I'm going to live!"

It was a powerful moment, and we were all silent as we took in this startling information.

But it was only years later that I came to realize my question to that child wasn't really my question. It was Jerome's, and therefore not authentic, at least not for me. I had used Jerome's "instant question." It had worked, I suspect, because Jerome's wisdom about children could shine through my own dim understanding, but it didn't equip me for any subsequent encounters. The danger with any teaching method is that the teacher can begin to rely on instant solutions, tricks that "always work" but are rarely understood fully. Unfortunately, some teachers cling to them like a life raft, never realizing that the raft has a slow leak! Eventually, the teaching becomes inflexible and even boring. When people throw out "I wonder" questions with no real, internal dialogue, it sounds "sing-song-y" and inauthentic. It reflects this "instant" quality of teaching, and exposes us for the frauds we have become, however unintentionally. We must do the inner work, for the sake of the children and for our own sakes.

What slowly began to dawn on me was that I had to find my own authentic questions. I realized this through the practice of dialogue in my own life.

Dialogue is not just conversation with others, but conversation that also happens internally. It asks the same kinds of questions of the self that you might ask another, in dialogue: "What is happening here? What feelings am I experiencing? How strong are they? Why are they happening?" *(Pay attention to your intentions. Notice your assumptions and inner voice.)*

And moving on to more questions: "What is the most important thing here?" Almost always, for me, the answer to this question in Godly Play is "The circle of children." My intention is to be true to my calling, to be in service to the circle of children, of which I am a part. So the next question is: "What do I want to have happen here?"

This question can be answered with integrity only when I have calmed my own feelings and mentally set in the midst of the group, like a fragile ball, the idea of "whatever is best for this circle of children." In other words, I have to get over any anger, frustration, hurt, feelings of revenge, need for control and anything else that will get in the way of doing "the best thing." *(Imagine the other person's perspective.)* And I have to do this in the space of a few seconds. So it takes practice, and it doesn't always work. Sometimes I really blow it.

Yet I've also realized that I can't berate myself for doing the wrong thing: for not understanding fully enough, or for not checking my own emotions completely. I can't always impart pure love to these kids. Only God can. It's okay for them to realize I make mistakes. As a matter of fact, it's *important* for them to realize it, so that they are free to make their own mistakes and learn from them. If we are authentic as teachers, mistakes aren't a problem. They offer more opportunities for learning or creativity. Last week, I brought the story of the Exile to the circle when the class informed me that I'd told that story to them the last time we were together. Oops. "I did?" Yes, I did.

"You probably want a different story this time, huh?" Yes, they did.

I looked over all the shelves. Finally, I asked, "How about a parable?" *Yes!*

I went to the shelves and looked at all the parables, considering each one, waiting for one to call to me. Dialogue helped me, because I wasn't uncomfortable in the silence. I listened, I waited for God to give me a good idea. The Good Samaritan called. I answered. It was a remarkable class that day. One question that we kept talking about was "I wonder if the original traveler would have stopped to help the Samaritan?" and then, "I wonder if he would stop to help someone after the experience of being beaten himself?" Good questions. Real, authentic questions. And good conversation followed. I listened, rather than panicked. I wasn't so concerned about looking foolish; instead, I listened inside for what was the next best thing to happen.

In dialogue, silence is necessary. Questions are considered and discarded because they are not ones that will improve upon the silence. Or because they aren't really questions, but rather just another way to say what *you* think needs to be understood. In dialogue, you talk less and listen more. And you listen in a different way; you listen to really, really understand.

So if a child asks a question that sounds strange, you ask a question back to try to understand, to clarify. The key is "to try to understand." In my experience, the remarkable, unfailing thing is that the children know the difference. They respond honestly and authentically when they understand that they are being questioned from a place of not knowing. They warm up to you. They appreciate your respect and authenticity.

I used dialogue one evening when a member of our youth group sauntered past as we were eating dinner at an outdoor cafe. The girl was pierced in so many places, it was hard to look without cringing. Her boyfriend had spiky hair, a nose ring, leather everything and an attitude. We called "hi" to them, and they stopped. She talked and when her boyfriend realized we were completely unfazed by his bizarre appearance, he joined the conversation as well. We talked and laughed, asked questions. They relaxed. It was a good exchange. It took a lot of internal dialogue, and openness. It took genuine interest and caring. It took thinking about what *they* might have been feeling, maybe expecting us to shun them. It took giving them the acceptance that all human beings want—and need.

Dialogue is the intuitive process that we use all the time as teachers in a Godly Play class. One Sunday, I was the door person. There was a boy in the class who was often disruptive because of his inability to sit still and keep quiet. The storyteller worked with him on being ready, but after several tries, she asked him to come and sit with me, which he did. I continued to watch the story and to listen. I noticed that he was still distracted, so I said very quietly, "Watch." He did. I noticed something about the story, which I told him in a quiet voice. I wondered something, and I told him that, too. He wondered back. When it was time for the response, we started to talk about the story, and what we had each noticed. A few minutes later, he was telling me that his older brother was really bothering him, hitting him all the time, making his life at home feel unsafe and unhappy. I asked him if I could mention it to his mom, and he said he wished I would. I did.

So where was dialogue in that? As I watched him in the circle, I was feeling more and more agitated. "This kid *never* seems to get it!" I thought. "He won't sit still, he won't be quiet, he bothers the other kids, he makes the storyteller feel inadequate to the task..." The thoughts went on and on. When she sent him to sit with me, my first reaction was to say something to make him understand how frustrating his behavior had been—in other words, to shame him. My better self told me to shut up. I realized, fortunately, that silence was the better part of wisdom. I looked at him out of the corner of my eye, and realized that he already felt ashamed. I realized, too, that this wasn't anything new for him. He was *always* getting in trouble with teachers. I told myself that my job here is to love these children, and this one needed my love more than anybody else right now. I kept silent.

The good girl teacher in me told me to watch the storyteller and the story, to be properly engaged, to "model" for him. I tried. I was still concerned more about him, though. I concentrated on loving him and asked God to help me in this situation. As I silently sat there, I began to wonder what the story had to do with us, right then, with him and my concern for him. When I spoke, the question came directly from that wondering. It was an authentic question, and it engaged his attention. Was it strictly according to the Godly Play model? No, probably not. But it was being in service to the circle of children, to that particular circle of children. And I could have gotten there only through using dialogue.

Last week, I went into one of our classes and this same kid was in there. He's a few years older now, and still finds it hard to control his behavior, but it's better. We started talking about the story of the great family, and about Sarah and Abraham who built the altars of stone because God was with them in the new places. I said I wondered about those altars, how they built them, and how big the stones were. He entered into it with me, and decided that the stones were *big* ones, hard to carry, substantial. He acted out carrying them on his shoulders, bending over with the weight of them. We laughed together. We are friends. I think we will always have a special bond because he knows something about me and the way I am with children and he responds to it. And because once, instead of making him feel guilty, I dug deeply into myself and asked for God's grace-filled wisdom and found my love for him.

I've come to understand that the only real answer is the one that responds in love to the real question. And if I don't have any real questions, I simply don't speak.

WONDERING AND THE RESPONSE TIME

by Becki Stewart

THE GODLY PLAY RESPONSE TO ART WORK

With Godly Play there is a paradigm shift from the traditional interaction with child about their work ("Oh, isn't that pretty," or "I really like that picture," or even "What is it?") to a descriptive respect for the child's work.

In Godly Play we are teaching children the art of how to use religious language to know God and find direction in their lives. Religious language, the language of Sacred Stories, Parables, Liturgical lessons and silence, requires us to confront the four existential questions that all people, even children, have. These questions are: What is the meaning of life? What is death? What does it mean to be alone? What does freedom really mean?

In a Godly Play classroom, we are helping children make meaning in their lives by giving them the language in the lessons and then allowing time and space for them to respond in a deep way. When children answer the wondering questions or make a response with clay or crayons, they are integrating this Christian language into their lives. For this reason, the child's *work* is viewed as a *highly personal response* to the language and to God.

What is going on is important *work*—asking and answering the existential questions of life/death, aloneness, freedom and purpose. We need to be careful to "remove our shoes, so to speak" when working with children. Their work, as are their lives, is holy ground.

The work of the children is what they give back to God in response to the lesson or the time spent in a Godly Play room. Children's work can be an answer to a wondering question, a sculpture made of wire or pipe cleaners, a painting, a story written in a People of God journal or even making the choice to walk carefully around another child's work or to help with the feast.

Children's work is a holy, sacred thing. Their work is given to God as a gift, a deeply personal response to the lesson. Jerome Berryman reminds us to treat it with *respect and creative energy.* As storytellers and door persons, we seek to support and sustain this creative process. We are always looking for ways to make connections to the Christian language.

CHANGES IN WORK AND RESPONSES

Children's work and their responses to the lesson change as they grow older.
- Young children (three- to four-year-olds) will not usually verbalize their thoughts or will say very little. They care more about learning or internalizing the story with their bodies by moving the story pieces or moving around the room, as well as learning how to be together in a circle. Also, figures in their artwork will be less recognizable and they will not be able to articulate their ideas or thoughts about what they made. Younger children will finish drawing or painting quickly and be ready to move on to the next thing. Part of their work is to learn to clean up and put things back: "Let's get it ready for the next person," "You can do it. Let me show you how."
- Older children (kindergarten through fifth grade) will usually be more verbal *in their responses to the wondering questions.* Repeat what you heard them say in your own words, giving them the opportunity to add more or to change their thinking. Try to encourage them to talk to each other. Value all responses. Ask "Could you tell me more about that?" Their work includes learning together in a community and taking care of the environment. We are helping them to move to a level of personal responsibility and independence in their responses.

Responses also vary according to individual tendencies. Some children are ready to tell you about what the lesson means to them immediately. For others, it is a private, more internal process. We can encourage responses from all during the wondering questions by waiting patiently (at least a minute or two before moving on to the next question so they have an opportunity to process the question and formulate a response) or by asking the question again. Sometimes putting your hand on a particular place or story piece will help elicit a response.

However, don't be afraid of silence in a Godly Play room. Be comfortable with it. We will never know what is taking place inside a child's heart and mind.

AVOIDING BARRIERS AND OBSTACLES

Be careful not to lessen or cheapen the work or to place any barrier that might impede it. Barriers include careless handling of work, speaking with sarcasm, giving your own interpretation, even asking children what they did, speaking too loudly or interrupting the work time. For some children, the fear of having to explain their work will keep them from attempting to work or approaching a teacher. Protect their right to respond and to share it with you. Sharing with others can be a scary thing.

Trust the creative playful Spirit. We are all co-creators. Honor God's presence and participation in the play and work of children. Honor the scared relationship between you as the teachers and the child.

HOW DO THE STORYTELLER AND DOOR PERSON SUPPORT ART RESPONSES?

A Godly Play teacher doesn't tell children how to feel or think about a lesson. They "set the stage," so to speak. They make a place in which the work can happen.

- We do this by making the time and space *safe*. Children share their work only when they want to. There is no pressure or structured sharing time in a Godly Play classroom. Sometimes their work is so private or personal that it not meant to be shared. When children do share, teachers need to be ready to receive a child's work without value judgement.
- We make supportive, but open responses to children's work. ("Hmm, brown." "I wonder if the birds are happy.") Open responses give children permission to tell what they want, not what you want to hear.
- We guide them into *"constructive expression,"* always making connections back to the language in the room. "We only have a little time each week to do work about the lessons here. You have all week to draw or make things about video games." "Can you find something in this room that goes with your work? Walk around and see if it fits somewhere. Why don't you bring that back to your place and use it?"
- Sometimes their work is themselves. Tired or cranky children may need the space just to sit, lay down or even go to sleep, if that's what they need. "Why don't you

go get a rug and rest? Make your work yourself today."

- Work for the day may be taking care of the environment. Have available a duster, dustpan and small broom. (Older children can also use brass cleaner and polishing rags.) As Jerome Berryman says, "The classroom is a small world. How will they learn to take care of the bigger world outside if we don't help them to be good stewards here?"

- Use descriptive praise rather than "I" statements. The work doesn't have value because the *teacher* likes it. It is valuable because it is the child's personal response to the lesson, a way of making the story his or her own. It is the way a child makes meaning with the language, continuing to create the relationship with the Creator and those close to them in the community.

- The adults should encourage responses, even for the reluctant child who doesn't know what work to do by saying, "You may not know what to do, but your hands know what to do." Or to the child who says, "I'm not an artist." a teacher can respond, "You do good work," or "It is your work, not someone else's. It is your work, and only you can do it."

- Model or demonstrate the procedure for getting work out and putting it away. This is done as a child needs to learn it, not as a separate lesson. Children are motivated to learn when they want to know something.

- Encourage independence and responsibility for work and materials, reinforcing the idea of making the language their own.

- Care for the work. Don't throw it away and don't lose it. Without saying a word, we communicate an important "unspoken lesson": children's work has personal meaning. The piece they have made may be about what matters to them about life and death. Work can be displayed in the room. It can also be taken home since the work belongs to them. When children move to a new Godly Play room or leave the church, wrap work up in a decorative gift bag and give it to them like a present.

- Have a respectful attitude.

- Carefully, thoughtfully organize the environment. Model careful handling and taking care of things in the room—another "unspoken lesson!"

- Trust that God makes us co-creators, that all people can respond to God and that God accepts all our responses.

HOW DOES THE ENVIRONMENT SUPPORT ART RESPONSES?

In a Godly Play room, we are surrounded by the stories of the People of God. We are immersed in the Christian language. The environment and materials for the lesson are active participants in the learning. They can say as much or perhaps even more than what is heard in the classroom.

"The environment shapes the learning." What the space looks and feels like is an important unspoken lesson. A well prepared, organized, pleasant room tells the children this is a good place to be, a place to do important work. A beautiful, well-cared for room says adults care about what happens here.

The Godly Play room should:
- contain *quality* materials that support quality work (brushes, paints, etc.)
- provide a variety of age-appropriate materials
- be organized so children can see and find what they need; a place for everything and everything in its place
- have child-friendly materials, tools and supplies, such as scissors that really cut and lids that a child can open
- be filled with colorful, interesting materials that call to the children
- support the creative process from start to finish (For example, clay work that needs to be baked requires a designated space in the room.)
- have a procedure for the storage of work not yet completed, work to be taken home, and a way to send work with a child when he or she moves
- support responses for the different and diverse modes of intelligence (For example, there can be materials to help children retell the story aloud, make a book, tell the story in the desert box, build a temple out of wood pieces or make up a song.)

HOW CAN WE USE TIME TO SUPPORT ART RESPONSES?

Time is a crucial element in a Godly Play room and another one of the "unspoken lessons." Be willing to let some things go for the sake of preserving the safety of the room. If you hurry children through the work time, they will never feel safe in investing the time to go deeply into the work because their experience has not been one of adequate time. Be prepared to make choices on behalf of the community of children. Be aware of the work going on in the community so you can make a good choice. For example, if they are deeply involved in the wondering time, you may decide not to do work that day or if they are deep in their work, you may decide to forgo the feast that week.

Respect "religious burning," the theological equivalent of David Elkind's "intellectual burning." As oxygen is critical to a fire, so is adequate time to learning. Without enough time to reflect and expand upon the lesson, less learning will take place.

Have *work days* when no lesson is presented. Work days include only the greeting and a feast. Children spend the rest of the session working with the materials or lessons they chose. Support this process and guide children by helping them remember work that is not yet complete or stories they may choose to retell. You can also help by reviewing possible work choices.

By the things we say and do in Godly Play, we help children use Christian language to make meaning for themselves. The unspoken lessons of caring for the room and allocating time are equally important in supporting children as they integrate these lessons into their lives.

> "We teach children to love this language, this community making and meaning making set of symbols used by Christian people; when we do that we have done something profound. If we teach children the art of how to use this powerful language to make meaning for their lives, we have done even more. What is most important, however, is to teach the children to know that they have inherited this profound way of being together and of making meaning. It was given to the Christian people, because they do count every one."
>
> —Jerome Berryman, *Teaching Godly Play*

RESPONSE TIME SUGGESTIONS

by Kathleen Capcara

WHY AVOID ASSIGNING CRAFT PROJECTS?

During the response time after a Godly Play lesson, children can choose to work with lesson materials to retell the lessons; read books, maps and other reference materials; write in journals; or work to maintain the classroom environment. But for many Godly Play teacher, the most challenging part of managing response time is the work with arts and crafts materials.

According to cognitive scientist Douglas Hofstader, most of our concepts are wordless—even though we try to describe them. Many children find it difficult to participate in the wondering questions following the Godly Play lesson. It's not easy finding just the right words to express what the story means to them. Sometimes only making an image or a physical object can help clarify the meaning of a wordless concept. Images transcend time and space, capture fleeting sensations and construct new ways of thinking.

Open-ended response projects can teach children to trust their own way of seeing the lesson so they can be receptive to God in all kinds of experiences. If we assign a craft project, we miss the chance to fully challenge children to enter the story and express for themselves what it means to them. So Godly Play response time is not about "doing a craft project, or even about "making art." A better way to look at the craft options in response time might be as "meditation with art materials."

But most children have been conditioned to respond to the sight of an array of art supplies with a sense of inadequacy. When they encounter crayons or paint or clay, they believe they must make something "beautiful." And they just don't feel comfortable enough with specific art materials to know how to use them effectively to express wordless concepts.

Godly Play teachers need to think about finding ways to show the children how to use art materials in a way that does not intimidate them, but rather allows them to explore the wordless concepts in the Godly Play lesson they just hear, or in another lesson that feels important to them. This may involve some extra talking about the lesson before sending the children from the circle to work on individual responses.

WAYS TO SPARK A RESPONSE

In Godly Play, we believe it is important for the children to choose their own work to do in response to the lesson. However, the concept of using art materials for coming close to God is different from the concept of using them to make a specific product. There *are* ways to open their minds to new possibilities in working with art materials without actually suggesting projects to them, ways that say, with or without words, "Your fingers already know the way."

- Discuss the visual elements of the lesson: color, texture and shapes. Talking about the gritty sand, or the dry wind of the desert, the cool oval, green leaves of the mustard tree, the fire and smoke of Mount Sinai, or the clear, wavy blue water of baptism may give the children some images to start with.
- Find a word or feeling that came from the children during the wondering, and suggest that one kind of work the children might choose is to make a collage or clay "sculpture" of that word: Celebration. New Life. Fear. Happiness. Some modes and vectors of deep body knowing suggested by Howard Gardner and mentioned by Jerome Berryman on page 39 in *The Complete Guide to Godly Play: Volume 1* may suggest images the children can work with.
  1. moving towards—backing away from
  2. wholeness—breaking
  3. empty—full
  4. stained—washed clean again
  5. opening—closing
  6. beginning—ending—beginning again
- Talk about colors and how the students might use them instead of images to express an idea or feeling from the story. For example, you might say to older children, "Some people use the names of colors to show how they feel. When people are sad, they talk about feeling blue. Or they say, I'm so mad, I'm seeing red! But maybe blue can be a happy color. Blue skies make me happy. And red sometimes makes me feel excitement. I think it up to you as you do you work to use colors in a way that helps you tell the story."

To extend response with art materials for young children with short attention spans:
- If children approach you with drawings that you think they may be abandoning before they are finished, you might want to try to draw out the child a little before encouraging them to put the work away. Say something like, "Look at all the shapes you have made on your paper! What other kinds of shapes can you make? Smooth? Wiggly? Bumpy?"

- If young children announce they are finished after just a few minutes, try to re-motivate them into continuing by introducing a different colored crayon or marker, a different sized paintbrush, small pieces of construction paper that can be stuck to their pictures or wooden craft sticks for working with clay. The children will either become involved with their work again, or they will put down one last dab of work, and say, "Now, I'm done."
- If they do the latter, it was done for you, not really for them. Children should feel they are working to please themselves, but sometimes if you show interest, it encourages them to discover both new ways to work with the materials and the joy of investing themselves more deeply in their work.

BEING IN "THE ZONE": A REFLECTION ON RESPONSE TIME

by Kathleen Capcara

When is the last time **you** were in "the white moment?" You might call it something different, but you know what I am talking about. I'm talking about the moments in your work or play when everything "clicks." When your skills are *so perfectly* suited to the challenge before you that you seem to blend with it. Everything just seems to come together, effortlessly and harmoniously. It's a beautiful thing.

Athletes sometimes call this state "being in the zone"; psychologists call it "flow." In flow, we are at our peak. The white moment, the zone, flow—whatever you call it— can happen in any kind of activity. Playing tennis or soccer, gardening, preparing a legal document, devising a marketing strategy, helping siblings or friends get over an argument, preparing to teach a class or planning a retreat—any activity can become a white moment. The only requirement is that our skills so perfectly match the demands of the moment that all our self-consciousness disappears. At that instant, attention is fully focused on the task at hand. One sign of being in flow is that time seems to pass more quickly. We are so attuned to what we're doing that we're oblivious to any distractions.

"After *three days* they found him in the temple." A white moment is what I believe let the boy Jesus and the elders in the Temple lose track of time for the three days Mary and Joseph were frantically looking for their son. Why else would *adult* teachers not insist that Jesus find his parents and tell them where he was? I think when he was twelve and in the Temple, maybe for the first time, Jesus felt everything "click." His questions and wondering about scripture were *so perfectly* suited to the challenge before him that he seemed to blend with it. As he spoke with the teachers, all that preteen self-consciousness disappeared. The teachers recognized someone in "the zone" when they saw it. And they were amazed.

When Mary and Joseph found their young son in a state of "flow" in the Temple, they seemed baffled. The Temple was the last place they looked! "Who is this young man?" they might have wondered. "Where did this love of scripture and discussion come from? As a carpenter's son, why isn't he interested in how the Temple was built instead of being captivated by the Torah?"

It is not always easy for parents and teachers to come to terms with the fact that no matter how involved we have been in shaping our children's beliefs and actions, much of who they are—their deepest selves—comes straight from God. Watching someone we know in a state of flow, which scientists have documented as the ultimate state of creativity, can be both amazing and unsettling. For people in flow are not concerned with pleasing us. They are in connection with their truest selves, functioning at their peak creativity and therefore in connection with God, the ultimate Creator.

As Jesus did, it is important for all of us, including young children, to spend some time in the white moment. Think back on the time in your childhood when you first realized that you were good at doing something, all by yourself, without the help of your parents. Was it drawing a picture, acting or dancing on stage, writing a story, solving a math problem, playing a sport? Remember how awesome and free and powerful you felt? It is often like that when we discover and live into our true selves.

As someone who spends a lot of time working with the children and youth in my position as a director of Christian education, I have seen many very young children begin to discover their true selves as they enter a white moment. That is one of the great joys of teaching Godly Play.

In fact, the brain wave patterns of children up to adolescence are different from adults. They are rich in the theta waves that enable people to naturally enter flow, the ultimate state of creativity. Flow involves *total absorption* in a task. We've all noticed that children have the capacity to get lost in what they are doing in a way that is much harder for adults. You know how it is when you take a walk with a child, only to have to pause for long periods while a pile of dirt or a leaf or a worm is examined at length. Godly Play teachers frequently have the pleasure of seeing children get "lost in a moment" as they go about doing the work they have chosen for themselves in response to the lesson.

I think holding onto the ability to get lost in the moment is one of the things Jesus was talking about when he said that in order to enter the kingdom of heaven, we need to enter it as a child. To be caught up in flow—to be transformed by an encounter with our creative God—we need the chance to stay with an activity for as long as it captivates our imagination, even if it lasts over days or weeks.

Unfortunately, our way of life does not allow much space for us to do this. Both adults and children are often over-scheduled, moving quickly from one activity to the next without much time for reflection and deep enjoyment.

In Godly Play, one of the most important directives is to let children "choose their work" in response to a Bible story or lesson instead of assigning craft activities. This is often the hardest thing for new teachers to understand. But letting children choose their response is important because over-directing a person can hinder his or her creativity and make it nearly impossible to achieve flow. People who are over-directed often feel too much anxiety about producing something that will please others. In order to find our true selves, and find the God-given gifts that will put us in a white moment, we need to be free to explore, to experiment, to be original.

So instead of focusing on the need to see children produce the right answer, or a craft that shows they "understand the lesson," in Godly Play we try to guide the children into the kind of quiet, personal response to the lesson that will invite them into the white moment. And the classroom time is structured to allow children to return week after week to response activities that captivate them.

I believe God wants us all to spend as much time as we possibly can in the white moment. God wants us to dwell in that place where our skills are *so perfectly* suited to the challenge before us that we seem to blend with it. Right now, it may be that not many of us spend a lot of time in flow, but I think the Kingdom of God is, by definition *the zone*. Everything we do there will seem effortless, harmonious and unified. It will be beautiful to behold!

I believe that sharing in wondering and response after hearing a Godly Play lesson within the circle of children is a way of reminding us that God created us to live in "the zone."

When is the last time you were "in the zone?" And when can you get yourself back there?

—from a sermon preached at Church of the Good Shepherd, Baltimore

CHAPTER 3
HELP WITH MANAGING SPACE

THE GIFT OF THE GOLD

by Kim McPherson

On the Sunday of the Epiphany story, I supplied each of my teachers with frankincense, myrrh and myrrh oil, and delicate, tissue-thin sheets of twenty-four carat gold. In our three- and four-year-old class, the children sat in the circle, transfixed as the storyteller placed the tiny stones of incense on the burning charcoal, and told of this ancient way of getting ready to come close to the presence of the mystery of God. They smelled the oil of myrrh and heard her speak in hushed tones of this strange gift, used when someone important dies. They reverently passed the sheet of gold, one tiny hand placing it in another, and they were puzzled to discover that bits of the brightly colored gold tissue had stuck to their fingertips. Sara, their teacher, wisely waited as each one made this discovery, and then she asked, 'I wonder where you could put the gift of the gold?" One child leaned into the circle, and then they all did, and they stuck their fingers full of gold onto the Christ candle. Where it still is.

GODLY PLAY ON A SHOESTRING

by Sally Thomas

GETTING STARTED

Very few churches have the kind of money they *wish* they had to implement Godly Play the way it's implemented in a church that's built up its space and materials over a matter of years. We need to remember what Jerome Berryman has taught us: a beautiful setting and a feast are really all you need to work together.

I've started Godly Play on a shoestring twice and I want to affirm that whatever you can provide will be a huge gift to the children. We adults might want perfection, but children recognize a gift that has been given. We will give a most valuable gift to them and to their families just by providing a space, a feast and a storyteller.

If you're going to start Godly Play anew, one of the best things you can do, regardless of how much money you have, is to take a break. Close the doors to the room. Close the shades. Put an announcement up on the door: "Something special is going on. We can't tell you what, but it's a present." You may share that it's Godly Play that's coming, but build the mystery. Spin a web that draws in peoples' attention. Play with it, make it kid-friendly: This is *fun*. Wrap up the door like a present, paint it red or put on polka dots on it.

SHARING THE SPACE

Most likely, you'll have to share the space set aside once a week for Godly Play. Don't worry; most of us do! You may need to box up your Godly Play materials each week and store them or even take them with you. I've kept mine in milk crates in the back of my station wagon.

Rather than engage in a "turf war" over the space, be an advocate for mutual respect in sharing the space. You'll find you'll have the best success when you present the Godly Play space as a sanctuary for children rather than a special kind of Sunday school classroom. Try to engage at least two people in the congregation who understand the work of Godly Play and can support you.

The best thing is to have your clergy leader on board, the one person who has the overall vision for the whole congregation. If that's not feasible, then you build a relationship with the vestry or other church elders. You may get more questions than support at first, but anything's better than a pat on the head that says, "How nice you're doing this for the children." That's a classic "unspoken lesson" that the work doesn't matter much to them.

Make sure the program does matter to your congregation. Build a network with trainers and other people in the Godly Play community. Even an occasional phone call with an experienced trainer can help. Within your own parish, remember that it doesn't cost anything to have a weekly phone call with your rector. It doesn't cost anything to do a presentation to the adult education class. It doesn't cost anything to leave an open invitation with the vestry. It doesn't cost anything to volunteer to take a story to the nursing home, or to make yourself available as a substitute speaker to fill in that last-minute cancellation for the parish program.

THE FIRST STEP

So how do we begin? The best way to show our respect for the children is by cleaning the space. Just clean it. Cleaning doesn't cost anything, but it tells children, "This space is a sanctuary for you. We care about you." So start by cleaning the windows and curtains. If necessary, give the room a fresh coat of paint. Fresh paint, fresh air and natural light will go a long way toward creating a beautiful space.

You'll want a rug to cover the floor and make comfortable sitting. Instead of an expensive patterned rug, I recommend a neutral-toned rug that won't cause apoplexy to anyone if it gets stained! Though expensive, wool is a good investment: it wears well and many parents prefer rugs without chemicals for their children. Try saving money by shopping at a carpet remnant place, but get the rug bound, if you can afford it.

THE CLEANUP

Next, before you buy *any* furniture, stories or supplies, ask for permission and help for a cleanup or "closet rescue" day. Every church has old materials: fabric pieces (for underlays), unused vestments and furnishings (for the church corner) and unwanted linens (for the baptism story). You'll need more prosaic items, too: baskets, pots for plants, napkins, plates, cups, file folders and trays. With luck, you'll turn up extra crosses, old maps, a picture of Da Vinci's Last Supper and felt board materials no one has used in decades.

That's why it's worthwhile to take time in setting up a Godly Play program. By doing such community-wide efforts, you'll enlist enthusiastic allies for the program—and your church will appreciate the spirit of stewardship shown in recycling beloved materials rather than straining the church budget to buy everything new.

One item you're likely to turn up in abundance is a wide range of books and story books, especially old Bibles. (This is a great activity to do with a curious child or group: pick up all the Bibles and place them in the middle of the storytelling circle. Ask: I wonder which one is the real Bible?) Keep a row of assorted Bibles underneath the Books of the Bible material in your room.

FIRST INVESTMENTS

Now that you've found what you can for free, what should you buy or make? I think the most important first item is a focal shelf—a three-shelf unit— to anchor the room. It should look beautiful, but it doesn't have to be costly. Inexpensive shelves can be painted or covered; even droopy shelves, if loved, can serve the purpose well.

There might be someone in the congregation who would enjoy making a shelf unit for the room. If so, ask them to put it on casters, to make it easier to move. If you don't have such a handy volunteer, start looking for inexpensive shelves. Melamine shelves are almost always on sale. These can work, although they do have the drawback of being not very deep. Materials placed on them might come a little too far forward. Remember that the focal shelf needs to be set apart somehow from all the other shelves in the room. It might be slightly higher or slightly wider; it might be made of natural wood instead of painted wood.

After the focal shelf, you'll also want a shelf unit on either side. Inexpensive furniture stores are fine resources for these. The wood can be finished or unfinished, as long as it is clean and not splintery. Everything else will fall into place around this basic setup.

I think the next best investment is a laminator. It's less expensive to laminate paper prints from Godly Play Resources or elsewhere than it is to buy wooden figures. I also find it easier to slide laminated story figures than wooden figures, which tend to catch on the felt underlays. However, too many trips to the office store for laminating can add up costs. A laminator, which you can buy on sale for $80-$100, will pay for itself almost immediately. You can laminate other high-use items, too, such as a checklist with instructions for the door person, a list of guidelines for observers in a Godly Play room and the "Ten Best Ways for Parents" found in *The Complete Guide to Godly Play: Volume 1.*

WORK SUPPLIES

After the basic setup, gather supplies for the children's work. You don't need to worry about child-sized tables or chairs, but you'll want a good supply of inexpensive mats or small throw rugs. Be sure to get them all at once so that they look similar; don't invite competition over room supplies.

Next you'll need cafeteria trays for children to work on. Some teachers omit these, but I think younger children find them helpful to assemble materials, and older children find them helpful to give a focus to their work. You can buy these at a restaurant supply store, or ask for a donation from a cafeteria-style restaurant. Our teachers got a donation from a local grocery store. Ask for a number of trays to match the number of students you expect, plus an extra five. If you get a donation, or if a supply store is willing to sell you some at cost, send them a thank-you note on your church's letterhead so they can deduct their gift as a charitable donation. If you can't get a donation, you can also find these at discount stores. Make sure that they stack nicely, and that they're made of smooth plastic.

When choosing art supplies, remember that "less is more." Children don't need fifty choices of art activities, and you don't need to offer every child every choice in the room. At the beginning of the school year, discount stores carry stacking plastic trays to hold hairpins and accessories. One of these 4" x 6" trays will comfortably hold a set of eight fat markers. Buy four identical sets of markers and store them in stacked trays. At my former church, we bought sets of markers in 1997 that they're still using six years later! When supplies are only used once a week, and cared for lovingly—with lids replaced each time—they last.

Buy four twelve-packs of crayons and take them out of the box to store in trays. You can also provide four sets of colored pencils. Place four watercolor sets in long, narrow baskets with one paintbrush and a little paper cup added to each basket. Be sure to provide a pitcher of water for paint cups.

For modeling material, play dough made from a homemade recipe is just fine—people can make it at home as a gift to the program. (See the box on page 45 for a recipe from Sally's sister.) Measure clay ahead of time, roll it into small balls and put them into tiny "zipped" plastic bags. Door persons can check and refill these bags each week. Children can keep items to dry on a special shelftop. Since children are process rather than product driven, often they care very little about taking finished items home.

That's plenty of art material, but you can add materials you like, such as "big" paints (tempera), glitter, real clay, etc. There are many wonderful art options, but many of them are too expensive for our program and perhaps yours: we only have $250 per year to supply two classrooms.

Do try to offer more sophisticated materials for older children, such as two sets of pastels and pads of good drawing paper, available at discount stores. Older children love Sculpey modeling material, which they can use to make more sophisticated projects, including prayer beads. Keep it on your wish list, and if you get a donation, roll it into 1" balls and keep them in tiny "zipped" plastic bags.

In every classroom we offer journals, which can be as simple as the inexpensive spiral-bound notebooks sold in three-packs with school supplies, at the beginning of the school year. Offer a cup of pencils or pens to accompany these. By keeping a set of blank books on hand, a child can take one and keep it in the "safekeeping" box or folder you provide for each child. Even when we have children who are one-time visitors to the room, we always make each child a folder. We tell these visitors, "You can take what you made home with you, but if you ever come back, this folder will be here for you and your work." These folders can be discarded manila folders you found in your church cleanup session, stored in a plastic milk crate.

Remember that work time for children can be time that they work on themselves, too, by lying down or sitting quietly alone. I use the yoga positions for the Sun Salutation to pray the Lord's Prayer; I keep photographs of those poses on a work shelf. I also have a miniature sacred labyrinth that sits on an old music stand near the work corner.

Children may work on themselves before they even enter the room. I find it helpful to have a mirror attached with suction cups outside the door of the room, at eye level, for the younger children. The door person can ask them to take a look at themselves in the mirror and make sure they're ready to enter the room.

BUILD THE STORIES

Next start to build stories for the room. Remember that if you set a big paper clip down in the sand and say, "That's the city of Jericho," children will go along. It's wonderful to have plenty of story materials made from beautiful wood, but you don't *need* them for Godly Play. It's especially important not to let their absence keep you from doing Godly Play.

CONTAINERS

When you look for containers for your stories, see if your closet cleanup turned up a good supply of trays or baskets. Make sure the baskets you choose are flat, without loopy handles, and with sides no higher than three inches. If you don't have enough of these, look for them at a craft, import or discount store, where they are frequently on sale.

HOLY FAMILY, RISEN CHRIST AND THE LIGHT

Begin with the stories that will sit on the focal shelf. For the Holy Family, you are likely to have found a creche set in the church cleanup. If not, your best bet for an inexpensive set would be to shop the sales after Christmas. The set you choose needs to be simple, touchable and not fragile. Try not to choose a set that is made from wood that is too lightweight. You want figures that will stand, not fall over, when you set them down. Make sure baby Jesus has open arms.

Instead of a cross, use a figure of the Risen Christ, such as the colorful Central American cross of the new creation, with the risen Christ on it. If necessary, you could use a laminated picture of the risen Christ. For the Light, try to find an inexpensive, unscented pillar candle. The altar guild may have an extra they can donate, but these tend to be too expensive to order for the classroom. You could substitute a regular taper candle in a brass candle stick, too. You can use a laminator to make clear cards to use as wax guards under the candles.

GOOD SHEPHERD AND WORLD COMMUNION

For a base, use spray adhesive to attach a green circle of felt to foam core. We laminated the paper print shepherd figure from the Godly Play Resources Parable of the Good Shepherd, then stood the figure up in a homemade stand. Ours was the cap of a flag pole, with edges cut into the side, but you could also use card holders or large black plastic binder clips with the metal parts removed. Put a dot of Velcro on the bottom of each stand, to help it adhere to the green felt circle. For sheep, we laminated paper print sheep figures from that same parable.

For the figures of the people of the world, we used the book *Design a Paper Doll You* by Phyllis Amerikaner (Learning Works, 1996). This book, available from a teacher's supply store or from *www.amazon.com*, gives patterns for designing paper dolls of every age, shape and race. Either have a party of people to make a dozen or more of these or just make three or four yourself, inviting children to add more figures as one optional work response.

BAPTISM STORY

You'll almost certainly turn up supplies for this story—a candle snuffer, a baptismal shell, a water cruet— in a church cleanup. Buy candles at a discount or party supply store; I recommend unscented 3" x 1" votive candles. Tea lights are too small and don't light well more than once. Don't let your materials set you up for failure!

For the oil, you can find tiny glass vials with black tops at container stores. Natural food stores carry essential oils, sometimes in inexpensive sample sizes. Use just one drop of scent, such as eucalyptus, to a small amount of clear mineral oil. Because of oil's potential to be messy, don't fill the vial more than half way.

DAYS OF CREATION

You can laminate the pictures for the Days of Creation or attach them to foam core. (For foam core pictures, have on hand one spray can of adhesive and one spray can of shellac.) You can draw the pictures yourself or use inexpensive paper prints available from Godly Play Resources. One beautiful option is to cut the designs from good quality construction paper or origami paper. I'm not an artist, but even my cut designs look beautiful—like a Matisse cutout!

These pictures are generally displayed standing up in a rack. You can look at kitchen or import stores for china display racks that would work well for displaying these pictures, as well as the pictures for Advent and the Faces of Easter (see below). Ask the store for any display racks they might discard over the year. You can find another inexpensive rack idea at craft stores. Look for unfinished wooden sleds, about 6"-7" long, intended for finishing by crafts people. If you turn one of these sleds upside down, there will be about 2" to 3" between the runners which can hold story cards.

NOAH'S ARK

If you can't turn one up, you can skip this story until later, but there are several options you can explore. Many toy or import stores carry inexpensive arks for children. I've told the story using a thin wooden hatbox for the ark, and little animal figures from a child's puzzle. You can ask parents to donate animal figures from a nature store; you only need six or seven pairs of animals. You may even find there's a family willing to donate an ark toy no longer used in their family. In addition to Godly Play Resources, another online resource for a wooden ark and figures is *www.wildapples.com*, which carries projects made by Vermont woodworker Gunther Wilde.

THE DESERT BOX AND THE PEOPLE OF GOD

You may be lucky enough to have a parishioner make a desert box for you, but until then, you could use a large plastic household container with a top. Whether homemade or store bought, fill your desert box with playground sand and put a potted plant roller underneath it to make it easier to move.

For People of God figures, you have several options. The simplest and cheapest option would be to use old-fashioned wooden clothes pins as people figures. Secondly, you could use colorful people figures from a rubber Lauri puzzle, found at quality children's toy stores. (Ask for puzzle #150.) The catalog put out by Lillian Vernon offers "People Dominoes," gingerbread people in different colors.

For the Ten Best Ways, I use a Valentine's day chocolate box as a container and use laminated cardboard for the commandments. You can simply use a big rock for the mountain, but you can also often find mountains and hills available in after-Christmas sales, in stores that sell materials to use in making Christmas village scenes.

Some stories, such as the Ark and Tent or the Temple, are labor-intensive projects for talented woodworkers. If you don't have such volunteers in your church, I'd recommend skipping these stories until later, when more funds are available.

ADVENT, CHRISTMAS AND EPIPHANY

As with the Days of Creation, you can laminate the pictures for Advent or attach them to foam core. Inexpensive paper prints are available from Godly Play Resources, but other options, including display options, are described above, under Days of Creation.

For the Mystery of Christmas, see the construction details in *The Complete Guide to Godly Play: Volume 1*. Remember that you'll need to use two copies of the book to make one set of materials. I bought used copies on *www.amazon.com*, because I felt better about cutting up used books rather than new ones.

For the Epiphany story, I like to burn actual pieces of real frankincense and myrrh. You can find these at stores that carry botanical or potpourri supplies, such as *www.herbco.com*. If you use essential oil, handle the oil as you would for the baptism story: use just one drop of essential oil to a small amount of clear mineral oil. Use a tiny vial and don't fill it more than halfway. Gold-covered chocolate coins are easily found in grocery or candy stores.

PARABLES

You'll need six boxes to hold the six guiding parables. Boxes exactly the same size are ideal, but if you need to use six different sizes of shoeboxes instead, that's fine. One possibility is photo boxes. In the little window provided for labels, we put a piece of colored felt to match the color of the parable's underlay. Photography catalogs sometimes carry sturdy archival boxes covered in copper or gold. For the parable figures, Godly Play Resources provides inexpensive paper prints. I prefer these prints, once laminated, to wooden figures, because I find it easier to move them on the felt underlays. You can find little wood accessories, such as small wooden birds, at the craft store but remember that parable figures must be flat, as if two-dimensional.

For the Parable of Parables, you'll want a set of nesting boxes available from container stores or from such catalogs as Lillian Vernon. For the Parable of the Deep Well, you can make a well yourself with self-hardening clay. You might find a small wooden bucket or dipper from a craft store; I use a tiny wooden watering can with the spout broken off.

For the parable games, Godly Play Resources provides the texts as xerox copies. You could also type these up yourself, using the texts provided in *The Complete Guide to Godly Play: Volume 3*, and print them onto gold paper before laminating them. If you adhere them to foam core instead, a nice touch is to use semipermanent gold marker as a trim on the edges.

LENT AND EASTER

For the Mystery of Easter, I use cardboard puzzles. Use a craft or utility knife to cut a cross from cardboard. Glue felt (purple on one side, white on the other) to the cross, then cut it into six puzzle shapes. Making one from wood would be a wonderful project for a church volunteer with a jigsaw. For the drawstring bag, you can sew a piece of purple velvet to a piece of white satin. The first time I made this story, I didn't have my sewing machine unpacked yet—so I used fabric glue to join the two pieces.

For the Faces of Easter, you can buy and laminate prints from Godly Play Resources. You may want a volunteer artist from your church to paint these, but keep in mind that this is a more challenging project than the woodworking projects. The artist would need to study the materials carefully, and come to a deep understanding of the vision that animates them. We want to be careful not to let what is personally important to each of us take over the metaphor conveyed; we want to pass on our shared theology, not make up our own.

OTHER STORIES

Some stories, such as the Synagogue and the Upper Room, are best deferred until funds are available to purchase them. The Circle of the Eucharist is easy to make, and preferable to make if the conventional materials don't reflect the actual liturgy of your church. The Journeys of Paul can be made in the same fashion as the Faces of Easter.

Finally, for the Books of the Bible, see if you can find a poster showing the Books of the Bible in your church cleanup. (Godly Play Resources sells an inexpensive poster, too.) You can do this lesson just using the poster, if necessary. Our parish library has a series of books with commentary on the Bible, so we went on a field trip to the parish library to present this lesson. Using a Books of the Bible poster, we made piles of the commentaries to match the groupings shown in the poster.

WELCOMING HELP

Remember that you are in a community with the members of your church. Enlist them as your allies, and you'll find that help is as close as the pews of your church. I've suggested projects for crafts people to help with, but you can also ask them to watch sales for you, to note when such items as clay for the older children, paints, baskets and other supplies go on sale. Someone who likes to sew can bind the edges of the cloth underlays with satin tape for a finished look.

Keep a wish list—prioritized and with prices given—of items you would welcome in your program: a laminator, a special Bible, a set of candles, etc. Even better than a list is a folder with a picture of each item accompanied by a note that gives the price and information on how the item will be used. Keep a disposable camera with flash in your room, so that whenever someone offers anything, even a box of tissues for the room, you can take a picture of the person holding it. Keep these pictures in an album and keep the album in the room, so that children can see for themselves all the people who have contributed to their room. This is a wonderful item to make, and it becomes part of the story of the room.

Some people will want to contribute funds, of course, and these are always welcome. Even if you have plenty of money available, however, don't spend it all at the beginning. Hold on to a portion of your budget because what you need will reveal itself over time. Stacy Williams Duncan, associate rector of St. James, Fremont, points out that because Godly Play is a program able to last over twenty years, some churches purchase supplies with capital improvement funds.

Finally, remember you are part of a community that extends beyond your congregation. I can make these recommendations not because I had everything figured out from the beginning, but because I made—and continue to make—all kinds of mistakes as I went along. Feel free to contact me or another Godly Play trainer for ideas. You'll find there's a whole community of us committed to helping one another build sanctuaries for our children.

JENNIFER FLOYD'S PLAY DOUGH RECIPE

Combine 2 cups flour, 2 cups water, 1 cup salt, 2 heaping tablespoons of Cream of Tartar and 1/4 cup cooking oil. Stir over medium heat. It will get hard, but keep stirring until it forms a ball. Let cool, then knead well. Store in sealed containers, such as zipped plastic bags.

GODLY PLAY ON A BUDGET: MAKING GODLY PLAY WORK WHEN YOUR CHURCH CAN'T AFFORD IT

by Kathleen Capcara

DEVELOP A SPONSOR-A-GODLY-PLAY-LESSON PROGRAM IN YOUR CHURCH

First, you need to tell a Godly Play story to as many adults as possible. Because Godly Play is a multisensory approach, the experience of hearing and seeing a lesson presented is essential in communicating the effectiveness of the Godly Play method.

Telling a Godly Play story to the vestry, session, parish council or other governing body, or presenting an adult education class about Godly Play are good ways of letting adults see for themselves how the materials draw the listener into the lesson and wondering. But the most effective way to reach a large number of adults is to tell a Godly Play story during Sunday morning worship. If possible, use larger materials so that everyone can see them.

Next, in a high-traffic area of your building, make an attractive display of a few Godly Play storytelling materials. Borrow them from another congregation if you don't have the money to purchase a few sets. Attach index cards to each set of materials with the title of the lesson and the cost. An example: "Your donation of sixty-six dollars will put this durable Parable of the Great Pearl in our four-year-old classroom."

You can use a color catalog from Godly Play Resources to provide visuals for the other lesson materials you would like to purchase. Make an index card for each lesson material you would like to have. This is a good project for a Christmas time "giving tree." Attach your cards, decorated with angels, to a Christmas tree, and encourage church members to include Godly Play on their giving list.

SHARE GODLY PLAY MATERIALS AMONG SEVERAL CLASSROOMS

Each classroom should have a Circle of the Church Year wall hanging, pictured on page 24 of *The Complete Guide to Godly Play: Volume 2*. You can make these hangings yourself, or purchase them from Godly Play Resources. For each classroom, you will also need a focal shelf with a Christ candle, a Holy Family set with colored cloths to match the colors of the church year and a Good Shepherd and World Communion set. Each classroom should also have materials for the children's work, materials for the feast and materials for cleanup. You can begin as Jerome Berryman did, with a few shelves made from cinder blocks and boards and gradually add higher quality shelves over the years.

After each room is set up with a wall hanging, focal shelves, art materials and cleanup supplies, you can buy or make one complete set of storytelling materials and rotate them among all your Godly Play classrooms. Simply schedule the lessons so that each classroom is teaching a different lesson on a given Sunday morning. The lesson materials will move from room to room as they are needed.

USE GODLY PLAY LESSONS SEASONALLY OR OCCASIONALLY

Begin by using Godly Play lessons and materials one Sunday each month and use your customary curriculum for the other Sundays of the month. Sometimes teachers and parents are overwhelmed by the thought of change in Sunday school, a place they associate as a steadying influence in our changing world. Using Godly Play less frequently can be a gentler way to introduce the method while being easy on the budget. Within a few months, most teachers ask to use Godly Play more frequently. You will then have advocates who can help you find resources to make Godly Play happen for the children year-round.

Or buy or make Godly Play materials for one or two seasons of the church year—the Godly Play Advent lessons (Lessons 1-4 and 6 in *The Complete Guide to Godly Play: Volume 3*) are designed to be used for the entire season of Advent, as well as on Epiphany day. The Mystery of Easter lessons (Lessons 2-8 in *The Complete Guide to Godly Play: Volume 4*) are for use throughout the six Sundays of Lent. This means you purchase or make only one set of materials that is used for many weeks. Some congregations tell Godly Play parables (found in *The Complete Guide to Godly Play: Volume 3*) as part of their theme for Vacation Bible School, another seasonal use of Godly Play materials.

INSPIRE PARENTS TO BUILD THE PROGRAM

Start with one Godly Play classroom. Begin with Godly Play for the youngest class. Continue with your customary curriculum for the other children. Most often, when the young ones are old enough to graduate to the "usual curriculum," their parents have discovered the joys of Godly Play, which motivates them to get together and find resources for another Godly Play classroom so *their* children will not have to miss out on the Godly Play experience.

WORK WITH THE FISCAL YEAR

You do not need to start the school year with a complete set of Godly Play lesson materials. You can begin Godly Play with an empty classroom, except for the focal shelves, work materials for the children and cleanup materials. Other lesson materials are brought into the room on the day the lesson is first presented to the children. This means you can add the lesson materials one set at a time. Many churches make or purchase materials for lessons presented from September through December from one fiscal year's budget, then purchase lesson materials for the remainder of the school year with funds that become available from the new budget beginning on January 1.

GROUP PURCHASING POWER

If your congregation has a person who enjoys "organizing," you may be able to save money by working with other churches in your area to do bulk buying of felt, art supplies, trays, cleaning supplies, baskets and other materials for your Godly Play classrooms. Don't just concentrate on churches within your own denomination; this can be a good ecumenical project.

If you don't have a list of local suppliers, check the Internet for sources. Use the words *wholesale* or *discount* in your Internet search to find suppliers in your area.

QUALITY SAVES MONEY IN THE LONG RUN

It will be easier on your budget in the long run to make or purchase materials that are beautiful, well-crafted and meant to stand the test of time. When making your own materials, choose high-quality papers and woods whenever you can. Remember that these materials will be in use for many years. And don't forget that Godly Play Resources makes high-quality lesson materials that last for decades.

SUGGESTIONS FOR BEGINNING A GODLY PLAY PROGRAM

by Becki Stewart

- Recruit a partner or two to assess the needs of the congregation or parish.
- Spend time becoming acquainted with the Godly Play approach and structure.
- Prepare a plan for introducing the Godly Play program to suit your congregation's needs.
- Introduce the program to the clergy, the staff, the men's and women's groups (a great resource for the making of lessons and materials), Sunday school classes (potential sponsors for lessons and recruiting workers) and parents.
- Begin preparing the room and gathering baskets, lessons pieces, shelves and art supplies. Make a wish list and post it or give it to committees and classes.
- Set up a plan for learning lessons and training teachers. Will you work together or practice alone and meet to polish stories? How will you communicate needs and areas for improvement? How will you assess your work together?
- Get the room ready.
- Recruit feast preparers.
- Make a schedule of lessons, perhaps for one semester at a time.
- Invite parents to view the rooms and outline the program's objectives and approach. Be sure to review the practical matters of late comers, dropping children off at the door, when to talk to teachers and waiting for the children to be dismissed. (See pages 20-22 in *The Complete Guide to Godly Play: Volume 2*.) Hand out wish lists and have ready a list of needed chores, such as feast help, room maintenance and making materials.
- Advertise the beginning of the program. Consider using a mailing and signs posted around the church.

CHAPTER 4

HELP WITH NURTURING RELATIONSHIPS: CONGREGATIONS AND PARENTS

IMPLEMENTING GODLY PLAY

In order to share more information with the congregation about Godly Play we began several projects. We produced a Godly Play Handbook which included what Godly Play is, how it works in a classroom, stories and pictures from the children and suggested books to read on children's spirituality. The handbook was produced in large quantities and made available to all the families and anyone else in the congregation who was interested.

Another way that we shared word of this ministry with others was through a "Godly Play Worship Service." Everything from the bulletin to the hymns and prayers related to Godly Play, to children and to families. This was also the day that fourth grade children received their Bibles. The service began with a processional led by children and families. They carried in a large papier mache set of the Holy Family, the altar cloth, candles and other items that belonged on the altar. One by one, beginning with the altar cloth, children and parents placed all the worship materials on the altar. A storyteller presented the Story of Noah and the Ark to the congregation followed by the four wondering questions which were printed in the bulletin. The congregation was given a short time to share their response to the questions with the person sitting next to them. I shared a short sermon on Faith Formation and the Work of the Children, and several of the teachers shared their thoughts on the experiences of working with the children in the classroom. It was a great service, well received by the congregation and significantly helped to further the entire congregation's understanding of Godly Play.

—by Kathy Meyer

ADVOCATING FOR GODLY PLAY IN YOUR CONGREGATION

by Kathleen Capcara

The Godly Play approach can appear radical to many people who are unfamiliar with its effectiveness and widespread success. Most adults instinctively feel that today's children should be taught the way they were taught. This can present a challenge to the educators who want to introduce Godly Play in a new setting. But if you take the necessary precautions in shepherding Godly Play through the hierarchy, you will be more likely to gain the support you need to begin using Godly Play in your situation. Here are the steps to making sure Godly Play is taken seriously as you present it. These guidelines apply when you are first beginning the program as well as when you are expanding the program by adding more classrooms or implementing Godly Play in other situations or other aspects of congregational life such as Children's Chapel or intergenerational events.

DO YOUR HOMEWORK

If you sense Godly Play will be perceived as "controversial," talk with the church education professionals in your area who are using Godly Play. You will be able to find some contacts through the Godly Play web sites. Don't forget to be in touch with educators in other denominations who are using Godly Play. Keep a record of what you learn.

PUT IT IN WRITING

Even if you are not in a situation where a formal presentation will be needed, design a brief proposal document, with bullet points explaining your ideas for Godly Play. The act of writing down your plan for Godly Play will help you articulate it when you talk with others. When you put your ideas in writing, mention the place or places that have successfully used Godly Play. Be sure to include a list of resources needed to implement Godly Play. (See the checklist on page 61 of *The Complete Guide to Godly Play: Volume 1*.) Write down a time line for implementing the program, the number of volunteers or staff required and the estimated cost of your plan for Godly Play. Include at least a sentence or two about the benefits of using Godly Play in your setting.

LINE UP ALLIES

Talk informally to the leaders in your congregation that you work with most often. This is better done one-on-one and face-to-face. Your enthusiasm and preparation will be best perceived in person. Use the telephone or e-mail only if the people with whom you are communicating know you well. Talk with parish leaders and those who have actively supported children's programs in the past. Present your idea for Godly Play and ask for their feedback. They may have refinements on your plan that will make it even better. Tell them your idea is in the beginning stages and may not be implemented, but ask for their support. Would they (or their families) participate in Godly Play?

PAY ATTENTION TO THE "SQUEAKY WHEEL"

Once your plan for implementing Godly Play has been refined and has grassroots support, use the proper chain of command to present your Godly Play program idea to the powers that be. Each congregation and situation will be different. Whether it is the pastor or rector, the Christian formation committee, the parish leaders or all three, present Godly Play to the right people in the right order. Many ideas have been rejected because of a failure to inform the most sensitive person first. If you don't know the right order, network with your allies to find that information out.

REMEMBER LEARNING PREFERENCES

Everyone has a preferred approach to taking in new information and to making sense of the information once they have received it. Use the written proposal you prepared if you think it will help. Individuals with a "concrete/sequential" learning style and visual learners will respond well to a written document. People who are "abstract/random" and auditory learners may like it better if you explain your ideas to them. Because Godly Play lessons appeal to people of all learning styles, it is always a good idea to present an actual lesson as a way of showing people how Godly Play works. You can often borrow one set of lesson materials from another church in your area for demonstration purposes.

If the "personal chemistry" is not right between you and a person key to the approval of your idea, consider asking someone you trust to present Godly Play to that key person.

HAVE A "PLAN B"

If you appear to be too attached to Godly Play in all its details, some people may be more likely to resist it. Congressional bills often end up with amendments tacked on to gain full approval of the Senate and House. Be willing to let your program idea evolve. The more people feel that they have contributed to the development of Godly Play in your congregation or setting, the more likely it is to be a success. However, don't give in on details of the Godly Play approach that you feel are essential. Remember that one or two people enthusiastic about Godly Play can begin using the program on a shoestring budget by starting small and growing gradually.

YOU ARE NOT YOUR IDEA

Jesus said a prophet is often without recognition in his own country. Try not to take it personally if your Godly Play proposal is not approved. Perhaps the time was not right. If you still feel Godly Play would do great things for your congregation or situation, you might consider sharing it with another professional as something to try in her setting. If it is successful there, you will have additional validation the next time you present Godly Play where you work.

THE MANY WAYS TO USE GODLY PLAY

by Kathy Meyers

INSIDE THE WALLS

- Sunday school (an entire Godly Play classroom, or a Godly Play story told as part of the learning experience in a Rotation Model classroom or any type of Sunday school setting)
- adult education classes
- worship services (sermon or children's sermon)
- church council meetings
- meetings for men's groups, women's groups, youth groups, parents' groups
- confirmation classes
- inquirers' classes
- intergenerational events
- retreats
- communion instruction classes

OUTSIDE THE WALLS

- senior citizen groups
- nursing homes
- hospitals and hospices
- prisons
- inner city neighborhoods
- homes
- extended family gatherings
- college and seminary classes

KEEPING GODLY PLAY FRONT AND CENTER: TEN WAYS TO HELP YOUR CONGREGATION REMEMBER GODLY PLAY

by Kathleen Capcara

DISPLAYS

Several times a year, display some Godly Play materials to keep the program fresh in the minds of the congregation. You might use a changing seasonal display in the church or parish hall entry space, centerpieces of different Godly Play lesson materials on tables at church dinners, a "card table display" at coffee hour, or a display near the church office or pastor's office. Some things besides lesson materials to include in your display are brochures, Godly Play books, photographs of the children at work (get parental permission before you display any photos of children), and posters with specific information about Godly Play, such as an outline of the class structure.

SERMONS AND STORIES FOR THE CONGREGATION

Often, a pastor will agree to mention Godly Play in a sermon, or tell a Godly Play story as part of the preaching. Some churches allow Sunday school superintendents or teachers to lead a "children's sermon" or preach to the congregation on occasion. If you feel reluctant to speak in front of a crowd in church, find a colleague to do it. This approach has the potential of affecting large numbers of people in your congregation who would not otherwise have the opportunity see Godly Play in action.

INTERGENERATIONAL EVENTS

Telling a Godly Play story with wondering questions and response time at an intergenerational event (Advent, Holy Week and Pentecost are possible times), is a good way to introduce Godly Play or remind the congregation that your program is alive and flourishing. Tell the story to adults and children together, do wondering twice—once with the large group, then a second time as the group breaks into smaller groups for making an art response. Often adults who are reluctant to talk about the story in a large group open up and offer valuable insights in smaller groups. For the intergenerational art response, you may want to offer one organized project as well as open response opportunities. For example, you could have materials for four small groups to make one banner for each week of Advent. In addition, have lots of paper, markers, scissors, paste and clay on hand for those who may want to make individual responses while others focus on group projects.

ADULT EDUCATION AND CONFIRMATION CLASSES

Many storytellers have reported success using Godly Play liturgical action lessons like The Circle of the Church Year, Holy Baptism and The Circle of the Holy Eucharist to adult classes. A hands-on introduction to the topic is a welcome change from the lecture format most adults experience in their own Christian formation. Sometimes adults who are introduced to Godly Play in this way have gone on to become storytellers and door persons in the children's Godly Play program.

OPEN HOUSE

Once or twice a year, polish up your Godly Play classrooms and invite everyone to an "open house." The beginning and end of the school year are obvious times, but also consider having an open house during a church fair or flea market, after a congregational dinner or on Easter or Pentecost, when you might not be having regular Sunday school. If your Godly Play classroom is not in an accessible area of the building, move the shelves and materials into a large space, where people can see and experience the range and scope of a Godly Play classroom.

GODLY PLAY STORYTELLERS AS "GUEST SPEAKERS"

Church committees such as committees for stewardship, the vestry, parish council, newcomers, music or worship, can benefit from a relevant Godly Play lesson as a prayerful and inspirational opening for a meeting. Offer this suggestion to the chair of the committee, then ask a storyteller to present the lesson during the first fifteen minutes of the meeting. Presenting a parable is one possibility: consider the "Parable of the Mustard Seed" for the newcomer's committee, or the "Parable of the Sower" for the stewardship committee. Using Godly Play in this way will introduce some of the most active members of your congregation to the program.

PRAYER BEADS

Use one wooden, glass or ceramic bead for each child in the class. Let teachers string them together into a necklace with a larger cross, shell or fish bead. The beads can be worn or carried as a reminder to pray for each child in the Godly Play program. One church asks Godly Play teachers to wear their beads to church on the Sundays they teach, so children and parents can easily identify Sunday school staff during worship and at coffee hour. Newcomers and other members of the congregation often notice the beads and ask about them, creating an opportunity to share the good news about Godly Play. Another church had each Christian education committee member string beads to take home as a reminder to pray for the Godly Play teachers and children.

VISIBLE PRAYERS

Write your own brief prayer for the Godly Play program in your church or use a formal prayer from your denomination's prayer book, such as a prayer for the care of children. Make pocket-size copies of the prayer on card stock for teachers, education committee members, governing body members and parents. Or find a calligrapher in your congregation to letter the prayer and display on a bulletin board in a prominent location in your church.

BANNERS

Ask children or adults or both to make banners from one of the Godly Play lessons, such as Creation, Advent or Faces of Easter. The banners will remind people of your Godly Play program whether you use them as part of worship or simply display them in the church or parish hall.

BULLETIN AND NEWSLETTER ARTICLES

If space is available to you in the Sunday bulletin or monthly congregational newsletter, write a series of one-paragraph "advertisements" about Godly Play. (See "Four Brief Articles about Godly Play," below.) Or you might list the lessons being told in each of your Godly Play classrooms on a given Sunday, or explain one aspect of the Godly Play approach, such as getting ready, wondering, the use of hands-on materials or the feast. Include a name or phone number readers can use to learn more information about Godly Play. If you write six to eight one-paragraph articles ahead of time, it may be easier for you to get them into the Sunday bulletin or monthly newsletter by deadline. These brief articles to keep Godly Play on everyone's "radar screen" can be recycled from year to year.

FOUR BRIEF ARTICLES ABOUT GODLY PLAY

by Kathleen Capcara

Use these articles as "advertisements" for your church school program. See the article above for suggestions.

GODLY PLAY: NO SINGLE WAY TO LEARN

(FOR THE BEGINNING OF THE YEAR)

Styles of learning vary as much as creative gifts. Some people learn most effectively when they see information written down, others when they hear it. Some people are kinetic; they need to move their bodies to learn. Some learn most effectively by working in small groups; others by concentrating on their own. There is no one proper way to learn; there are only individual styles of learning. Godly Play respects those differences.

In Godly Play, our Sunday school program for children ages _____, we tell stories with multisensory materials to appeal to a broad range of learning styles: *auditory*, because the story is spoken out loud; *visual*, because the handmade wooden figures represent what is happening in the story; *kinesthetic*, because the storyteller moves the materials around. Later, any child who wishes to learn to tell the story can respond in the same style.

In the "response time," those children who work best together can pair off or form groups to work on creative projects. Those who work best alone have the time and space to concentrate on projects by themselves.

We gather the children in a circle for the storytelling, and at the end for a feast, because they thereby learn about being in community and working together. Everything we do in Godly Play contributes to learning. To learn more about Godly Play and how to register a child you know in our Sunday school, call _____.

STORYTELLING AS SPIRITUAL FORMATION
(TO PROMOTE A GODLY PLAY CHILDREN'S SERMON)

Teachers and preachers all know that a good story makes listeners more receptive and inspires them to deeper and more personal learning. When the students are fully engaged in a lesson, teaching becomes a pleasure, rather than a challenge or a chore.

In a Godly Play classroom, it is common to see all the children gathered in rapt attention as the storyteller invites them to enter into the story themselves. The storyteller uses handcrafted objects of great beauty and simplicity to focus attention on the central elements. In the process the story comes alive again in the children's experience, helping them to find meaning in their own living — in what happens at home, at school and in the larger world. To see and hear a Godly Play story, attend our family service on Sunday, _____ or call _____.

GODLY PLAY: MULTISENSORY ENGAGEMENT
(TO PROMOTE A GODLY PLAY OPEN HOUSE)

When you look into the Sunday school classroom(s) in our church, you may notice many interesting items displayed on the shelves. In Sunday school for children ages _____, we are using a method of Christian formation for children called "Godly Play. The objects you see in our Godly Play classroom(s) surround everyone there with religious language, with the stories and symbols of faith. These sacred objects made of wood, fabric and wicker invite children to touch, feel and enter into the stories. Moreover, having beautiful things designed by adults for them makes it clear to the children in a tangible way that their religious education is important to all of us. To see all our Godly Play lesson materials, come to the open house after our Stewardship breakfast on Sunday, _____ or call the Godly Play Program Coordinator at _____.

TIME AND SPACE FOR GOD'S PRESENCE
(A MIDYEAR REMINDER ABOUT GODLY PLAY)

Children today experience as "normal" challenges that were unimaginable to many of us in our youth: the increased violence on television and on our streets, the high rates of divorce and remarriage, the rapid and destabilizing pace of technological change. We ourselves are frequently bewildered and frightened by the world we live in; imagine how unsettling it must be to children.

Setting aside a regular time to be still in the presence of God and the learn the stories of faith is essential to a child who needs a sense of being surrounded and upheld by God's love. Among the things we can offer in Godly Play, our Sunday school program for children ages ___ are the stories of the Bible and the religious traditions that have sustained people's spirits for generations. These stories are a means by which children can learn to cope with the anxieties generated by the world around them. And they will be able to take comfort in a growing awareness of the long history of God's loving presence. Our Godly Play classrooms are always open to new students. Bring a child you know to Godly Play, held every Sunday morning at _____. For more information, call _____.

GODLY PLAY OBSERVATION GUIDELINES

by Sally Thomas

Note: Keep a laminated copy of these guidelines in each Godly Play classroom, to use when an adult visits or observes the classroom.

Welcome!

Dr. Jerome Berryman, an Episcopal priest, has spent over twenty years observing and interacting with church school children in a "Montessori" fashion. Godly Play is the result of that research. Observation is the most valuable tool to learn about the program and we are glad that you are here.

As an observer, please:
1. Sit quietly in the chair offered and do not move around the classroom.
2. Do not engage the teacher or children in conversation during the class. This is the children's work time. (If a child approaches you, please explain that you are watching and redirect them to a teacher if they are seeking help.)

3. We are always around before class and at the fellowship time; we would love to answer questions and hear your thoughts then. If you have negative feelings, please share them with the teachers. We do not have the ability to cast an objective eye on our own work and welcome all feedback.

Thank you very much for your cooperation. These guidelines are suggested to help ensure the least amount of disruption during an observation. We want you to see the children in their routine.

Schedule:
• Getting Ready
• The Story
• The Response Time
• The Feast and sharing time
• Dismissal

Please do not be offended when you are not offered "the Feast." You will see that the focus stays within the circle. Breaking the circle distracts the children and can be confusing for them. By staying apart, you can truly be a "fly on the wall."

Remember: Children are oriented to process, not product. It is important to appreciate and watch what they are doing, not the finished product.

DON'T FORGET THE PARENTS!

by Kathy Meyer

When we first began Godly Play our thoughts focused on the children and the teachers. We were concerned about finding teachers who really understood Godly Play and would be able to develop a classroom built on respect for the child's experience with God. We did hold an open house for parents and children before Sunday school began, but that was the extent of our relationship with the parents. After a few weeks parents began to ask questions and were very curious about what was happening in the classroom.

Since we were just beginning with Godly Play there was much to do and we still weren't focused on the parents. In response to a request for "take home" information, I began to develop a sheet for families with a picture, scripture and wondering questions for the story told each Sunday.

As we began to think more about the parents and how to include them it became clear that Advent might be a good time to invite parents to come to the classroom and be a part of the circle. Each teacher developed an area in the classroom that would serve as a backdrop for a large nativity scene. There were many creative ideas:

some brought in straw while others made background scenes. Invitations were sent to parents and children and they were asked to bring a special holiday treat to share during the feast.

On the special day, parents and children arrived together and all sat in the circle, or parents sat behind their child if space was limited. Children and parents experienced Godly Play together as the storyteller told the Advent story, and then led the group in the wondering. After the wondering, each person was given a bag of homemade Kool-Aid play dough and families worked together to fashion figures for the nativity scene. When all the figures were completed, we sang "Away In A Manger" as each person placed their figure on the straw in the prepared nativity scene. It was such a beautiful, quiet, collaborative moment that everyone shared together. We were all truly blessed by the experience. Then we all shared together in prayer and the feast as we took a little time from the serious "getting ready" of Advent to celebrate together as God's people. The Advent "scenes" were saved and put on display in the church library so that everyone could enjoy them, and the event was so successful that plans were made to offer a similar event during Lent.

As time went on I began to see just how important parents are to the work and success of Godly Play. A pastor asked me to come to her church and work with her to teach Godly Play to parents and children together. We set up a class that met on Monday mornings for eight weeks. Moms and children came together, sat in the circle and experienced the story. While the children had response time, Moms worked on making story materials to use at home. When they were finished with the story materials we offered classes on children's spirituality. Moms then joined their children in the circle for prayer and the feast. It was a wonderful experience for everyone. The pastor felt more connected with both the parents and their children, and the parents enjoyed participating in this spiritual experience with their child.

Another experience on my journey helped me to fully realize how integral parents are to Godly Play. I was invited to a family camp to present a two-hour workshop to parents on Godly Play and the spiritual development of children. This was to be followed later in the day by the presentation of a Godly Play story to the children. In the parents' workshop, I presented The Parable of The Good Shepherd. The parents were intrigued and wondered how their children would respond to it.

When the time came to present the same parable to the children, it was early evening and they had experienced a full day of play. They knew nothing of Godly Play or sitting in the circle and they were not used to "getting ready". It was a large group of children of mixed ages. I began by leading them through some getting ready suggestions such as "quiet your toes, your feet, your legs, your body, your arms, etc." Then I presented the Parable of the Good Shepherd, followed by wondering questions and a response time with three or four choices available. Telling the story to the children was difficult from my perspective because it was hard for them to settle down, and during the wondering some of the older boys were trying to show off rather than really wondering.

To my surprise, though, the parents were excited about the whole experience and how well their children had responded. They thought it was great and they were amazed at how well their children had sat in the circle and been involved with the story. It also made a huge difference that the parents had seen the story earlier in the day. They were involved, they knew what was going to happen and they were interested in how their children would react to the story. It felt as if we had become partners in nurturing the children's spiritual growth.

All of these experiences, and more have taught me how significant the connection between church and home is, and how important it is to involve the parents at the very beginning so they can actively participate in the process of knowing Godly Play and deepening the learning experience at home. I believe that when we begin a new Godly Play program, we need to begin with the parents. They need to experience a full Godly Play session so that they can understand for themselves the value of this way of learning. Then parents can begin to "know" Godly Play and learn how to use the stories to nurture the faith of their family at home.

A PARENT'S REFLECTION: GODLY PLAY IN THE HOME

By Sue Lundholm

Godly Play has been an important part of the faith life of my family and my extended family for the last three years. I guess you could say it has been a family affair for us. I am a storyteller and my son Joshua is the door person in our classroom. Josh and I have learned, played and grown in faith together with groups of preschoolers. We have shared many special moments experiencing the simple yet profound faith of children. I have taught Sunday school with traditional curricula in the past and I find that children respond to the Bible stories taught with Godly Play in a more thoughtful and meaningful way.

My son Andrew has experienced Godly Play in Sunday school for the last two years. My husband John also gets involved. He willingly becomes my "circle of children" as I practice the stories at our kitchen table, using canisters of spice and the salt and pepper shakers to represent the characters in the story. My Dad became involved, too, when we called on his woodworking expertise to cut over a hundred "people of God" and other materials for our Godly Play classrooms.

I'd like to share two stories about how we have used Godly Play in our home life and devotions. Two years ago while we were visiting my Mom and Dad for Christmas,

Mom asked me to do the devotions for our time together around the tree before opening presents. Our tradition has been to read the story of Jesus' birth from Luke, sing a carol and have a prayer. Needless to say, for the kids, our two boys and my sister's three children, the devotion time was elevated to a level of near torture as they impatiently eyed the pile of packages under the tree. I decided that I would use the Godly Play Advent and Christmas story for our devotions.

Since I hadn't thought to bring the materials with me, we made it a family project to gather the materials for the story. We used figures from the nativity set, my nephews' toy animals and my mother's candles. During our devotions that year, the children and I sat in a circle on the floor with the adults in an outer circle of chairs. The story unfolded with candles being lit for the prophets, the holy family, the shepherds and the wise men as we all journeyed together to Bethlehem. We were all anticipating, but it wasn't the presents we were waiting for. With all four candles lit, it was time to light the Christ candle and place baby Jesus in the manger. Jesus, the light of the world. Jesus, our savior. In that moment, presents were forgotten as we all reflected on the true meaning of Christmas. Since that year, my family has a new tradition for Christmas devotions.

Another way that we have used Godly Play in devotions at home began after I attended a seminar led by Jerome Berryman. One of the stories Jerome told was the story of Jonah. I have always liked that story because it is such a wonderful example of how God never gives up on his willful and often disobedient children. As Andrew was getting ready for bed that night and we were about to say prayers he scolded me for being gone all day on a Saturday and asked what I had done. I told him a little bit about the day and all the wonderful stories I'd heard. Then he suggested I tell him one of the stories before we said prayers.

So there in the quiet of his room, Andrew's blue quilt was transformed into a stormy sea, a box was the boat and Andrew's hand became Jonah. As I told the story and Jonah was flung into the angry sea, my hand became the great fish that swallowed Jonah and later spit him back onto the dry land. After Jonah preached to Ninevah and the people repented, my hand became the vine that shaded Jonah as he pouted because God had spared the people of Ninevah. As we shared the story, we marveled at how much God loves us and persists at making us His own. After that evening, we often told a Godly Play story together at bedtime.

CHAPTER 5

HELP WITH NURTURING RELATIONSHIPS: TEACHERS AND CHILDREN

STANDING IN THE MOMENT

I teach a Godly Play class to the second graders at St. Richard's Episcopal School in Indianapolis. One day, about a month after September 11th, a little girl in the class stayed behind when most of the rest of the class had left for their lunch period.

"I need to tell you something," she said matter-of-factly, looking from side to side at the girls on either side of her.

"All right," I replied, and waited.

She became slightly nervous, and then more agitated, looking at the other girls.

"I need to talk to you alone," *she said.*

I asked the others to leave, and she began.

"Last weekend, we went to visit my dog's father. We got him at this place out in the country, and we were going to visit him. But when we got there..." At this point, she was beginning to cry, and the words came out in choked sobs. "When we got there, we found out that he was dead."

"I'm so sorry," I told her.

By this time, she could not speak, but tears were streaming down her face. She gained control and continued. "It was a muskrat that killed him. Something like that, a small little animal. A small animal killed that big dog. I don't understand it!" By now she was shrieking out the words, "I don't understand how that little animal, with...those... sharp...pointy...little teeth could kill that big, strong dog!"

I realized then that she was talking about the United States of America, and Osama bin Laden. As we all were, she was questioning how our secure world could have been breached in such a huge and terrifying way by just a few, violent people.

I didn't understand it either. I could only stand in the moment with her.

—by Kim McPherson

TEACHER TRAINING AND AFFIRMATION

by Kathy Meyer

When we began using Godly Play we also began monthly meetings for the story-tellers and door persons. The meetings were built around the idea of the small group approach. I would meet with the small group leaders and then they would each facilitate a small group. At each meeting there was prayer, conversations about experiences in the classroom and a time of practicing the stories to be presented next.

This approach worked very well for the storytellers. They like the opportunity to share their experiences together and learn from each other. It was less successful for the door persons because they didn't come regularly and didn't feel as connected as the storytellers did.

We also held one day retreats twice a year for the Christian education committee at an area retreat center, and a yearly retreat for the teachers.

One of my greatest joys in this whole process was visiting with the teachers after class on Sunday mornings. The conversation often began with the words, "Do you know what happened today?" This was followed by the telling of a wonderful experience that children and teachers had shared together. It was such a joy to see the teachers delight in their experience and hear the amazing things that were happening in the classroom!

AN INTERVIEW WITH TWO TEACHERS

by Cindy Bishop

BIOGRAPHICAL INFORMATION ON PAM AND BILL NELSON

The Nelsons were married at Church of the Incarnation in February of 1968. Pamela and Bill have two grown, married sons and a four-year-old granddaughter. Since 1995, they've lived downtown near the Farmer's Market in a converted building.

Bill rides his bike to his job at the Dallas Zoo where he has driven the monorail since 1990. Earlier, he had a career in data processing. Bill sings in the choir and plays the accordion.

Pamela is a practicing artist, involved in public art at several Dallas Area Regional Transportation stations and at the Dallas-Fort Worth Airport. She currently serves on the U.S. Commission of Fine Arts in Washington, a four-year presidential appointment. She started an art program at the downtown Stewpot and has been a yoga instructor at local YMCAs.

Have you taught Sunday school before? If so what was that like and how does that experience compare with Godly Play?

Bill: Yes. It was fun but not as structured as Godly Play. I like a routine, and I think the kids like to know what to expect as well.

Pam: We "taught" three-year-olds. I remember mostly the days we used glitter.

Why have you chosen to teach in the Godly Play program? Why the youngest children in particular?

Bill: I watched Elizabeth Clarke present the Parable of the Good Shepherd and I was blown away into the fifth dimension. I like the young children because they are so funny and alive.

Pam: Bill asked me to join him in a great adventure—something we could do together. We don't work together on too much.

What part of teaching or working with the children do you like best?

Bill: Without a doubt it's the hugs.

Pam: I enjoy their openness and getting right below the surface quickly. They are transparent.

What part of Godly Play do you think is the most important?

Bill: The discipline of "getting ready." Having to be still and quiet. The prayers at the feast.

Pam: I think listening, and then responding is a great lesson. Learning to respect the space of others. Praying from the heart.

What things have you learned that have been helpful to your own spiritual formation?

Bill: When I prepare a story I always learn something: maybe the colors of the church year or the liturgy of baptism.

Pam: To come to God as a child. I watch how they do it.

Bill, what has been your favorite Godly Play story to tell and why?

Bill: The one that stands out in my mind is Noah's Ark or the Flood. It was my first story and I was very nervous. But when I stood up and held the ark up as high as I could reach, I heard some of the children gasp and I knew something was working.

Do you have any other comments?

Bill: I believe everything a person needs to live a good Christian live is covered in Godly Play Level I, for three- and four-year-olds. All the subsequent education is either a review or superfluous. We have the sacraments, the New Testament parables and the Old Testament stories. To be entrusted to present this material to fresh and nimble minds for the first time is daunting.

Pam: I was a child at Incarnation—Sunday school, church and vacation Bible school. It made a huge impact on my life. Perhaps one of these children will feel the same.

WHAT I LEARNED FROM GODLY PLAY

by Kathy Meyer

How to:
- know God beyond just learning *about* God
- live and work together in the community of the circle
- probe scripture
- discover and use the imagination God gave me
- take the time to enjoy the process
- appreciate and welcome the silence
- live in and care for the environment
- do the work of the people (liturgy)
- listen to others
- celebrate together in community
- tell stories of the Bible in a creative way
- pray individually and with others
- share
- show respect for others, even when I don't agree with them
- wonder
- build relationships with God and others
- think deeply
- enjoy the safety of an environment designed to nurture growth and learning
- know and appreciate the seasons and colors of the church year
- become more aware of the mystery of God's presence in my life

DISCOVERED BY GODLY PLAY

by Kathy Meyers

There was a day when I discovered Godly Play, and there was another day when Godly Play discovered me. I know when I discovered Godly Play, but I'm not sure when Godly Play discovered me. It has been a process that continues to deepen as time goes on.

It all began ten years ago when I attended an ELCA Lutheran Learning Ministries weekend event at a retreat center. The focal point of the event was the silent worship service we all participated in. It was a powerful experience, and a new one for me. A few days later I had a conversation with an acquaintance who had also been at the retreat. We talked about the experience and how for some participants it was very powerful and for others it just didn't "connect". He mentioned a new book called *Godly Play*, and said that one of the components in this "godly play" was silence.

It sounded very intriguing so I purchased a copy of the book and dove right into it. I was fascinated by the whole concept and wondered how it would work in our church setting. One of our Sunday school teachers, a woman who was also on the Christian education committee, read the book, too, and found it very interesting. I remember that she was interested in the gold parable boxes and wondered how they would work with the children in her class.

During this time I also connected with another Christian education director. She discovered that Jerome Berryman was offering a parable seminar in Houston. The seminar was held in April of 1993 and we were there, three women trying to learn what this Godly Play was all about. I remember that I loved the stories Jerome told—they were amazing!—but I was most intrigued by the segment on classroom management taught by Jerome and his wife Thea.

I had been a kindergarten teacher for several years before I began work as a director of Christian education; in my first year of teaching I had thirty-six children in each class. I became adept at managing and moving children from place to place but it was difficult to allow much freedom in a classroom with so many children. My limited experiences with Montessori had not been very positive so I was surprised to learn how children could learn to live and work well in the classroom, especially for an hour on Sunday morning.

I learned a lot at that conference. Actually I was on overload with all that I learned. Before the conference I remember thinking as a typical Christian education director, "I'll go, pick up a couple of new ideas, bring them home and use them". Well, I came home with a gigantic headache! So much of my thinking had been turned upside down and inside out that it took some time to process it all. Eventually I began to realize that this way of learning and working was what I had always been looking for.

Finally, I didn't have to write, rewrite or adapt curriculum to fit. This was complete and it was all we needed.

I also had to give up some favorites such as planning and directing the children in how to make a picture or create an art project. As a kindergarten teacher I had been trained to prepare learning projects that centered on art. I loved planning and carrying out the projects with the children, and hanging their art work all around the room. I especially enjoyed the seasonal projects. During Halloween, for example, the children would use orange paint to paint a pumpkin on their paper and then after the paint dried they would paint black facial features on the pumpkins. I can still see all the wonderful variety of pumpkin pictures hanging on the wall.

When I began working with Godly Play however I began to realize that if I just supplied the children with the art materials they could create their own work in the way that was most meaningful to them. It was a great learning experience to discover how to *support* the children in their work rather than *direct* them.

Prior to learning Godly Play I had wondered about how we might tell stories using small props and figures. In fact, I had ordered some storytelling materials that included small plastic figures and directions for making houses and villages. I had also wondered if somehow Barbie dolls could be used to help tell the stories. A few years later when I shared these early ideas with a group of colleagues, one replied, "We're glad you discovered Godly Play!"

The Sunday school teacher who had read *Godly Play* was very interested to hear of my experiences in Houston. She intuitively understood this work, prepared the parable of the Good Shepherd and presented it to the Christian education committee. They all liked the story and the concept of Godly Play very much The decision was made to begin it in the four- and five-year-old classes that fall, which we did. It went very well.

We then began thinking about the five-year-olds who would soon be in first grade. We wanted them to be able to continue the Godly Play experience. In January of that first year we began an experiment in the large fellowship hall where Grades 1-3 met in learning centers. We began three Godly Play circles, one for each class. There was a storyteller and a door person for each circle and they operated as though they were each in their own classroom. This worked well but, of course, it meant that we needed more materials and places to put them. Since the classrooms were multi-purpose and we didn't yet have fold-and-lock cabinets, we used carts to wheel the materials in and out each week.

It was a good beginning for these classes. It worked well to have the groups in their circles but we felt that regular classrooms would be even better and would offer a way to have a complete Godly Play classroom. The following year we added a class for three-year-olds and a class for Grade Four. This brought us up to seven classrooms in three years! There were many who helped get the materials together. Our custodian made all the parable boxes, another family spray-painted them, a grandfather cut out all the sets of the people of God and two woman who were doing community service at the church cut fabric and helped in numerous other ways.

The Christian education committee had grown from three to thirteen very involved and committed people. We met twice a year at a retreat center for planning and spiritual growth, and we held a yearly retreat for the teachers. There were monthly meetings of the storytellers to practice the upcoming stories and share with each other their experiences with the children. We were continually working to make our classrooms better, and to learn and grow in this ministry.

I had the opportunity to coauthor a teacher enrichment book on "Liturgy and Learning in the Classroom" with one of the friends who had traveled to Houston with me. Jerome came and presented a weekend seminar on the Liturgical Action cycle, and my husband and I taught our daughter's third and fourth grade class for two years. We envisioned our church becoming a place where we could offer workshops and share this wonderful work with others. It was an exciting time. Unfortunately, it didn't last.

Into the midst of all this wonder and joy there came a political agenda that was like someone throwing a can of ugly paint on a beautiful work of art. There were only a few people supporting this agenda but they had a loud voice. What had been a wonderful experience became a time of pain for many people. One storyteller who loved Godly Play went home in tears. When I called her later that night her husband said she was on the bed crying and he hadn't heard her cry like that since they lost their first child.

It was a very difficult time!! The storytellers decided that they would each take a turn writing an article for the newsletter about their experiences with Godly Play, and they did a wonderful job! We did a Godly Play worship that was very well received. As it often is with difficulties in the church most of the members didn't know what was going on; only a few people really knew what was happening. The heavy-handed agenda of the few continued until finally, several months later, I decided that it would be best if I moved on. It was very difficult to leave. I loved Godly Play, and I loved the wonderful, godly people I worked with.

I wasn't sure what to do next. There was so much grief and loss of dreams in this experience. I devoted a lot of time to my family, homeschooling my daughter and taking care of my mother who came to live with us. A very good counselor helped me journey through the days and months of pain. I finished my master's degree in human development and my wonderful friends from the church came to cheer me on when I presented my colloquium.

One day I received a call from the Youth and Family Institute asking if I would meet with a woman who was coming from England for a conference. She wanted to learn about Godly Play and Catechesis of the Good Shepherd. (I also have been trained in the 3-6 level in Catechesis of the Good Shepherd.) We began an e-mail correspondence and a few months later I met Rebecca Nye. We had a great time visiting a Godly Play classroom, attending a Catechesis training session and getting to know each other. Two years later when Rebecca was invited back to present a workshop and be a keynote speaker for another conference she asked me to present the weeklong workshop with her.

It was a great week, filled with learning and fellowship. One of the participants in our workshop was a woman from California, Sally Mancini. Sally had just been to a Godly Play teacher accreditation and she brought me up to date on everything that was happening with Godly Play. I reconnected with Jerome and was later invited to attend a trainer workshop and become a trainer. Rebecca and Sally have also become Godly Play trainers.

I'm currently working in a church as Director of Children and Family Ministries. The journey there has both surprised and delighted me. A great deal of spiritual ground-work was laid before I arrived and there has been an openness to Godly Play that is exciting. It is now the season of Lent and we are telling the stories of the Faces of Easter in all the Sunday school classes and the pastors are using the same stories as the focus of their weekly sermons. There is a lot of excitement in the congregation that everyone is hearing the same story each week, and families can go home and talk about the story they all experienced. We also just received a foundation grant from the church to build a Godly Play classroom that will offer a weekday class for parents and young children. This will be an outreach ministry to the community.

Recently, while working on my writing for this volume, I have reconnected with some of the storytellers at the church I worked at ten years ago. It has been wonderful to renew those friendships and hear about their families and what is happening in their lives. Another very interesting piece of information is that after all these years Godly Play is still being taught at this church and although there have been changes, a few of the teachers I worked with are still telling the stories! God is truly in this work.

The line from the baptism story, "The Holy Spirit goes where it will. It rides the invisible wind like a dove, and comes to us when we need its comfort and power," speaks to me in so many ways. I am continually amazed and delighted that out of chaos and pain God sent Rebecca, a kindred spirit, all the way from England to bring me back to this work. I am so grateful to be a part of this work. God truly does know the desires of our heart and continually surprises us by grace, even in the midst of pain.

THE GOOD SHEPHERD, GODLY PLAY AND A BOY LOST AND FOUND

by Cyndy Bishop

A family in our parish adopted a child several years ago. I'll call him Michael. Abandoned by his birth mother, Michael was found sleeping on a park bench. He had been wandering from place to place, surviving as best he could, for who knows how long. Fortunately he was found and later adopted by a wonderful, loving family.

Our church, the Church of the Incarnation, began a new approach to Christian education, called Godly Play, shortly after Michael's adoption. Godly Play centers on storytelling. It has three categories of stories: sacred stories from the Bible, stories from Jesus (parables) and stories about liturgical action. Godly Play uses hands-on materials to represent the characters and the scenes of the stories, allowing children to use their imaginations and to put themselves into the stories. For example, the Parable of the Good Shepherd is told on a felt underlay. There are felt pieces for a sheepfold, for the "cool, clear, refreshing water" (blue felt shapes), and for "the places of danger" (black felt shapes). A flat wooden figure carrying a sheep on his back is The Good Shepherd. There is also an "ordinary shepherd" and a wolf.

The first Godly Play story Michael heard was the Parable of the Good Shepherd. After hearing it, instead of choosing art materials, he chose to work with the story materials during his response time. For the next several weeks, when working with the materials, he would move the pieces to tell the story without saying the words of the story. When it came time to move the sheep into the dangerous places, he would let the sheep stay in the dangerous places for a long time. He would simply watch the sheep in the dangerous places. Perhaps he was remembering his own experiences of abandonment; perhaps he was contemplating, praying. Who can really know? Eventually, he would move the sheep to the safety of the Good Shepherd. As the weeks progressed, Michael chose to work with the story of the Good Shepherd less often.

Recently, the story was told to his class again. After class he told his mother that the Good Shepherd wasn't just good, but *great,* and that the ordinary shepherd wasn't just ordinary, but *bad*.

While Michael's story may not seem typical, all children face existential issues: fear of death and loss; alienation or being alone; the desire for and the fear of freedom and the need for meaning and life purpose. Many times we deny that our children have these existential issues and our denial may lead children to suppress their thoughts and feelings. Godly Play takes seriously the spiritual nature of children; it speaks to their emotional and spiritual needs. As Jerome Berryman, the creator of Godly Play writes, "Godly Play teaches reliance upon a gracious God who is real and accessible in all the mystery of life, both sad and joyful."

MAKING EXCEPTIONS WITHIN THE CIRCLE OF CHILDREN

by Sharon Greeley

One Sunday morning a couple of years ago, a woman with a very clingy six-year-old girl appeared at the Godly Play door. They were new to the congregation. The woman looked distraught and the child, Olivia, looked terrified at the prospect of being dropped off in this new place. It would be a few minutes before Godly Play began so I invited them to look around the room and gave them a brief explanation about Godly Play.

When it was time to begin our session, the woman asked if it would be possible for her to stay and attend with Olivia. Now, we try not to over-adult the Godly Play environment, but my intuitive sense told me that I needed to make an exception in this case. So, they joined the "circle of children" and Olivia held tightly to the woman.

After church, I heard their story. They had recently moved to the area from another state. The woman was Olivia's grandmother, and she and the grandfather were assuming custody of their granddaughter. All of their recent transitions had been very difficult for Olivia, and as a result she had become very shy and emotionally upset. The grandmother wondered what she could do to assist in her granddaughter's adjustment to this new worship space.

I had an idea. The "circle of children" had not seemed disrupted by Olivia's grandmother's attendance. What if she came with Olivia each Sunday and gradually moved away from the circle? We decided to give it a try. The next Sunday, she sat directly behind Olivia in the circle. Then, each subsequent Sunday she moved a little bit farther away from Olivia until she sat near the door. The next day, I received a phone call from Olivia's grandmother saying, "Olivia told me last night that I don't need to come with her to Godly Play anymore!"

One of our primary goals in Godly Play is to create a safe environment where each participant can come close to the presence of God. Stability and continuity are important factors in maintaining a safe space. An extra adult in the room could create an unstable environment, but I have also learned that we need to make exceptions for some children. We make exceptions for all kinds of personal challenges, whether they are physical, mental or emotional. When we do this within the "circle of children," we are not only creating a safe space but we are modeling how we live in community.

GODLY PLAY WITH OLDER CHILDREN

by Kathleen Capcara

Many people feel that using the Godly Play method with children between the ages of eight and eleven is too challenging for the average Sunday school teacher. Although older children require a slightly different approach, this age group can flourish within the structure of Godly Play. Because children in upper elementary school are beginning to develop abstract thinking, the wondering among this age group can be profoundly gratifying for the teachers and the children. And because of their more developed intellectual curiosity, creativity and skills with art materials, the response time can be more fulfilling as well.

In different times and different cultures, children of eight to eleven years old would still consider themselves to be just that—children. But partly as a result of the marketing mentality of advertisers in our current culture, children between these ages have come to be regarded as "nearly teenagers," and often feel they are too sophisticated to engage in anything called "Godly Play." With attention to detail, these prejudices can be overcome and you will likely find your Godly Play classroom for fourth and fifth graders to be more successful than many traditional Sunday school classrooms for older elementary students.

USE OF STORYTELLING MATERIALS WITH OLDER CHILDREN

Many people who embrace the use of materials in presenting Godly Play lessons to children ages three through seven begin to question the use of such materials when the same children are around eight years old and begin the third grade. It seems to be the age when many believe it is "time to put away childish things." Yet the same learning styles and preferences present in young children persist into adulthood. With older children, just as with younger ones, auditory learners respond to the way the Godly Play lesson is told, visual learners enter the lesson more easily because of the use of materials in presenting it and kinesthetic learners are fascinated with the way the materials are moved by the storyteller as the lesson progresses.

Maps, charts, graphs and other visual aids are used with older children and adults in various learning situations. Ideas and important points are listed on newsprint or dry-erase board. The use of storytelling materials in Godly Play is simply a more developed use of visual aids to teach the art of religious language and guide theological reflection for older children.

The most important thing for a Godly Play teacher of older children to remember is that the children will adopt your attitude about the use of materials. If you believe the materials are important and hold them with respect as you present the lesson, the children will consider this to be standard practice. If you feel somewhat doubtful about the value of presenting lessons with materials to older children, this will be communicated to them in subtle ways through your vocal inflection and body language.

It may help to explain to both skeptical older students and their parents who say lesson materials "are for babies" that we use materials so that we don't have to hold the entire lesson in our minds. This is like the materials used in a game of chess. Many adults play chess with beautifully designed chess pieces. What happens in a game of chess can be extremely complicated and the materials are not for babies. In fact, they help adults remember an elaborate series of events, or "moves" that take place during the game. In chess, the use of game pieces allows the players to step back and look at the entire progression of the game. In Godly Play, the use of lesson materials lets the storyteller and children step back and reflect in deeper ways because they can see the whole story laid out before them.

BEGINNING GODLY PLAY WITH OLDER CHILDREN

The first few weeks of Godly Play with older children can set the tone for the whole year. For people in your congregation who are skeptical of the effectiveness of Godly Play with older elementary school students, the first few weeks are critical. It can be helpful to consider carefully the following aspects of Godly Play:
• orientation
• use of language
• choice of lessons
• selection of materials for individual response during the first six weeks of class

ORIENTATION TO THE CLASSROOM ROUTINE AND ENVIRONMENT

It is a developmental characteristic of children ages eight through twelve to test limits and routines by challenging and criticizing the storyteller or the class rules. One way to get around this tendency is to help the children work with you to establish norms for behavior when you are together in the Godly Play classroom.

Instead of orientation, you might consider talking about the "great commandment" of Jesus found in Luke 10:27—love God; love your neighbor as yourself—as a prelude to guiding the community of children toward developing their own set of "norms" or "classroom rules." You may want to have the great commandment lettered in calligraphy on a beautiful scroll to keep in your classroom and to show the children as you talk about it. Or perhaps one of the students will work on lettering the great commandment during response time. Some older children also like to write out and decorate the classroom rules to be displayed in the room. Whatever approach you use, older children will be more likely to manage their own behavior if the entire circle has a hand in developing expectations for working together.

Other aspects of orientation can include introducing a prayer for the class to learn and say together as a way of "getting ready" for the lesson, such as a prayer from your denomination's prayer book or an appropriate prayer from another favorite book. In some older elementary Godly Play classrooms, every few weeks children take turns bringing in and leading a prayer.

Other classroom rituals for getting ready can include having the children put on a wooden cross necklace as they enter the room, take turns lighting candles and changing the underlay on which the Holy Family sits when a new liturgical season requires a different color.

CHOICE OF LESSONS

It is important to present many of the core Bible stories used throughout Godly Play again with older children, who are developing more sophisticated ways of thinking and talking about those stories. However, you may find it more effective to devote the first six weeks or so in a classroom with older children to presenting lessons they have never heard before. This may be a good time to present such lessons as the Prophets, the Parable of Parables, the Parable of the Deep Well and the three parable synthesis lessons. Jesus and the Twelve, the Circle of the Holy Eucharist, the Synagogue and the Upper Room, Paul's Discovery and the Holy Trinity are all lessons that have particular appeal to older children, perhaps partly because of the uniqueness of the materials. These stories circumvent the use of wooden figures or gold boxes that older children associate with the Godly Play lessons used when they were younger.

Object box lessons (see page 13) are intriguing for older children. You may want to start in September with a series of object box lessons about saints and conclude with several "work sessions" during which the children can create an object box based on their name saint or a favorite saint. This project could take several weeks for the children to research and implement and might conclude with an All Saint's Day intergenerational celebration using the lessons the children have written.

LANGUAGE WITH OLDER CHILDREN

The way you speak with older children and the way you listen to them is especially important in the first six weeks of class. Children this age are on their guard against any hint of being treated "like little kids." As with Godly Play at any age, children need to know they are seen to feel safe. In the beginning—the first eight weeks—they especially need to be recognized when they do what is expected. Both the storyteller and the door person should work hard at seeing and noticing each child in the room. Talk to the children about what you see.

In the first few months of Godly Play, the most important work of classroom management is to instill expectations, routines and skills that allow the children to take care of their own environment, learn to focus their attention and choose their own work. Comment positively on what you see, by reinforcing and redirecting the children. They will hear what you say and begin to learn to work from internal motivation.

The tone and language you choose will encourage children to work on their own and with competence. With older children especially, you many find a matter-of-fact tone to be most effective. Sometimes a hint of a playful attitude in your manner is helpful. Make appropriate comments that support the children's efforts and name a behavior specifically without calling it "good" or "bad." Spend most of your time noticing what the children do right. As the year progresses, you won't need to do this as much, but here are some suggestions to start.

"I notice you are waiting patiently for us to begin."

"I see you are really trying to write neatly in your journal. It looks hard."

"Martha and Rovan wiped the paint off their trays before they put them away."

"I see some legs sprawled in the middle of the circle. I wonder if anyone has seen what will happen to the juice if we don't sit up straight?"

MANAGING RESPONSE TIME WITH OLDER CHILDREN

You will first encounter the strong gender identification characteristic of older elementary students as they cross the threshold and find their own places in the circle. You will probably find the girls on one side of the circle and the boys on the other.

This tendency coupled with a stronger development of peer relationships among students between the ages of eight and twelve can make the wondering and the response time challenging to manage. But the critical thinking skills and creative skills of older elementary students can make wondering and individual response time the best part of your Godly Play class.

Remember Howard Gardner's eight "multiple intelligences" when you are setting up a Godly Play classroom for older children. Students with verbal/linguistic, logical/ mathematical, visual/spatial, musical/rhythmic, body/kinesthetic, interpersonal/ social, intrapersonal and naturalistic/classificatory intelligences can all be supported in a Godly Play classroom. If it is in your budget, pay particular attention to "bottom shelf" materials that support and deepen the stories you will be using for the first two months. Maps, charts, puzzles and reference books will be particularly appealing to older students with linguistic, spatial, naturalistic or logical/mathematical interests.

At this stage, as older students begin to respond more intensely to peer pressure, they also want to fulfill gender stereotypes. For example, many boys will tend to avoid art activities during response time. "Arts and crafts are for girls," they will often say. Having a variety of bottom shelf materials will help some older children respond to the lesson in other ways until they are comfortable with working with art materials to make a creative response.

Some art materials are less threatening for older children who are beginning to fear inferiority and feel reluctant to take the risk of making an art response. Clay, wooden craft sticks, wood scraps and materials for mask-making are most popular with people of all ages who feel they have no talent for making a creative response to a Godly Play lesson.

It is also an advantage that many older children have a heightened interest in working in small groups. If one boy develops an idea for response time, his participation can be instrumental in bringing others along to help with a big or extended project, like building a model of Solomon's temple with wood scraps and glue or making a relief map of Jerusalem with clay.

MORE IDEAS

DEMONSTRATE THE ART OF "BRAINSTORMING"

If two or more older students want to work together to make a project about a particular Godly Play lesson, it is a good sign that the community of children is taking on its own life. That is an important goal of Godly Play. Many small groups of children can work together peacefully, negotiate the roles of each member and create a response that satisfies all who participate without any intervention from adults. But in some cases, you may need to show a small group of children some effective ways to work together.

Suggest they list three parts of the lesson that made the strongest impression on them, to see if they have shared ideas about the lesson. Remember the wondering questions "I wonder what part of the story you liked best?" and "I wonder which part of this story is the most important part?" The students can then write for a few minutes in their own journals about what came to their minds as they were listening to the lesson. The next step may be to list images that come to mind from the writing and sketching them in the journal. Some questions to ask are "What feelings come to your mind when you look at what you wrote? (Or as you listened to the wondering questions?) "What colors come to mind? What shapes?"

But try not to be too directive. Remember that the most successful response-time work is chosen by the children themselves rather than assigned by the teacher.

HAVE A "BACKWARDS DAY"

Sometimes, just to keep things interesting, my Godly Play class of fourth and fifth graders will ask to have "a backwards day." To them, this means having the prayers and feast first, then finishing up work from previous weeks, and ending with the lesson and wondering. After six years of experience with Godly Play during Sunday school, the children enjoy the feeling of ignoring the routine class structure and "working outside the box" from time to time. But don't try this too often—what makes it fun is the fact that we don't usually do it this way.

STARTING GODLY PLAY WITH FOURTH AND FIFTH GRADERS

by Cyndy Bishop

We have had wonderful success here at the Church of the Incarnation using Godly Play with the three-year-olds through third graders and we are excited about expanding our program to include fourth and fifth graders. In fact, some of the Godly Play materials involve so much analytical thinking and synthesis that they are particularly suited for older children. Most of the Godly Play trainers I know work in churches that use Godly Play up to fifth grade and sometimes even higher. I recently communicated with another Godly Play trainer, Di Pagel, about her work with older children. Di is the director of Children's Ministries for Layfayette-Orinda Presbyterian Church. One of her most experienced teachers, Kathleen Krentz, sent me some of her thoughts.

"Older children," she said, "have rather rich spiritual lives about which their parents may be unaware or under-aware. As a culture, we don't always provide a way for children to wonder about God's presence. After all, it cannot be taught the way multiplication tables are taught. To know God, we have to experience God, and I truly believe that Godly Play allows older children to continue to experience and explore God in a safe, supportive environment so they can continue to grow in faith."

Kathleen had the following examples to share: a nine-year-old who observed that Bartimaeus' blindness could be a metaphor ("He was blind in his heart,"), and a ten-year old in a divorced family who observed that the commandment of faithfulness to one's spouse is so important because it is the children who are hurt the most in divorce. "Never in all the years of traditional Sunday school teaching," she said, "did I hear children reflect on God in their lives, in their worldviews, this way."

In my experience here at Incarnation with first through third graders, some children shy away from the discovery method of learning involved in Godly Play, but only for a short time. Much of their school experience, as fine as it has been, often closes the door to the open-ended, divergent thinking that Godly Play calls for. What a joy, however, when they start to feel safe enough to explore their own ideas and their deepest questions about God and faith. It's much easier for a child if someone gives them the instructions and materials for a teacher-directed craft, rather than asking them to explore their own feelings and ideas through art or storytelling. The path of least resistance is one we often choose for ourselves.

Similarly, during the wondering time in Godly Play, when children are asked to wonder about a story, or contemplate, they are also asked to do higher-level thinking: "What is the most important part of the story? What part could we leave out? Who are you in the story or which part is about you?" Sometimes both children and adults would rather just be told the answer. It is easy and comforting. However, it can also be frustrating to be given the answer or insight before discovering it on your own. If a child discovers something on her own, it is hers to keep; it becomes part of her spiritual identity. Knowing something intellectually is only part of knowing it spiritually. Many people grow up in the church fairly aware of what the church teaches yet they do not really *know* it spiritually, and as adults, they leave the faith. Godly Play seeks to inform the child's spirit as well as his or her intellect.

Di interviewed one of her students whose family is moving out of state. He took part in Godly Play from age four to fourth grade. She asked him if he ever got tired of hearing the same stories repeated. He laughed and said "Oh, no. I've seen Star Wars I don't know how many times and I always find something new. What I'm trying to do now is make sure I can tell all of the stories by myself. That way I can take them with me." He then asked her if he could tell her one of the parables. Then he asked to tell another. "I'm wondering," he asked "if when I come back here maybe I could be a storyteller?" Truly, this is my hope for all of our children—that they will make the stories their own, so that they can bless others with the stories of Christ, faith and tradition. Godly Play is providing our children a foundation for spiritual growth so that they will meet life's challenges with spiritual maturity.

OLDER CHILDREN AS STORYTELLERS

by Sharon Greeley

Our congregation began sharing the stories of Godly Play a few years ago with a core group of about seven children, ages three to eight. Currently our average Sunday attendance is about twenty children, ages three to thirteen. Plans are being made to begin a youth program next year for our older children, but not because they are bored with Godly Play. We are excited that we have a group old enough to move on to a new program where they can build on the foundation of the stories they have heard in Godly Play. Meanwhile, these older children continue to come and rehear the stories.

Our Godly Play session takes place concurrently with the "Liturgy of the Word" of the 10:00 a.m. worship service, and then we join the families for Holy Eucharist. Last year, some of the older children decided that they would like to meet at 9:00 a.m. for Godly Play because often they participate in the service as acolytes or choristers. Thus began a journey of a small number of older children gathering to go deeper into the stories.

Godly Play and other faith formation programs for children have created a paradigm shift in how we perceive children in the church. We no longer look at them as empty vessels to be filled but as viable members having the ability to lead us into the presence of God. I have been fortunate to share the circle with these God-bearing children.

One of my first experiences with their leadership abilities occurred three years ago. It was a Sunday morning in March. I was exhausted after having moved into a new home the day before. As we gathered in the circle, I told the children about my move and that I was not prepared to tell a story. Before I could tell them that we were going to have a "work day", one eight-year-old boy asked, "Can I tell a story?"

Surprised I asked, "What kind of story?"

"Oh, it's a story about God," he replied.

He then began the familiar words, "There was once someone who said such amazing things," and proceeded to tell the Parable of the Mustard Seed. He did not bring the story materials to the circle, but simply told the story from memory. This may be because he is visually challenged. All of the children listened attentively.

When he finished, another child raised his hand and asked if he could tell a story. This child, also eight years old, got up from the circle and brought the materials to tell the story of The Exodus. The other children were as attentive and focused with these child storytellers as they had been for any adult storyteller. I was overwhelmed with joy and awe as I sat there and observed these children share the stories. They had made these stories their own! And I realized that if I had been prepared that day, I would have missed this discovery!

This year I wondered if any of these older children who attend the 9:00 a.m. session might like to be storytellers at the 10:00 a.m. session. They said yes! We decided they would be the storytellers during the presentations of Parables. Each participant chose which parable he or she wanted to tell. They took home a mini-parable box to practice and then we all practiced together at the 9:00 a.m. sessions.

Our 9:00 a.m. session became like the practice sessions at training workshops. Those who chose not to tell a parable would work with one of the storytellers, offering tips and encouragement. When ready, the storyteller practiced telling the parable with the whole group and I led the debriefing. Most of this time simply focused on talking more slowly and with more volume. These children knew the parables by heart and how to ask the wondering questions.

I was amazed at the commitment and dedication these young people gave in preparing to tell the stories. But, the most amazing part of this experience was the depth of wondering during the practices. They genuinely responded to the questions, wondering with the storyteller, yet not looking to me for answers. They pondered, "Why did Jesus compare the Kingdom of Heaven to a loaf of bread?" "What really is the Kingdom of Heaven?" "I believe that the Kingdom of Heaven has no wars!" "I believe the Sower wanted the birds to pick up the seeds so they could carry them to other places." "Isn't Iraq our neighbor?"

At the 10:00 a.m. session, I welcomed our storyteller for the day, and we exchanged places in the circle for this part only. Each storyteller began with, "Watch where I go to get this story" and ended with the wondering. The circle of children focused on the story and responded to the wondering. They all did good work!

GODLY PLAY AND SPECIAL NEEDS CHILDREN

by Cindy Spencer

Over the past three years, I have wrestled with a growing awareness that my youngest son, Joel, has some special needs. He's always been slower than his older brother and sister in terms of his physical and social development, but it has become increasingly clear that these weren't issues that he was just going to grow out of. Specifically we have learned over the past year that Joel has epilepsy; amblyopia (lazy eye) with attendant vision difficulties such as difficulty with depth perception, focusing, tracking and fine motor skills; and most likely Sensory Integration Disorder, in that he does not process tactile information correctly, and therefore often interprets sensory stimulation as threatening.

Transitions are difficult for Joel, as is participating in groups with other children. School has been a challenge, but church school has often been a downright disaster for Joel, his classmates and his volunteer church school teachers. He spent a year in the three-year-old room screaming! In my dual roles of parent of this wonderful, mixed-up child, and the coordinator of children's ministry at my church, I find I need ways to make church and church school a safe place for both Joel (now six) and his peers, those "normal" and those with other special needs—a place where they all can experience God and explore what it means to be part of God's great family. I must also equip and support my church school teachers unless I plan to teach all the classes myself!

There are many aspects of Godly Play that make it a helpful environment for all children, but especially for children with special needs. The consistency of the classroom structure is very important for any child who has difficulty with transitions. The balance of time spent hearing the story, and time spent working, either with the story or with art materials, allows children to make choices about the ways in which they learn best.

A parent session at the beginning of the church school year can invite parental understanding of the class structure as well as give the parents familiarity with the language used in a Godly Play classroom so that they can help communicate to their children about what to expect. The parent session could also provide good opportunities for inviting parents to give information regarding the needs of their specific child. Allowing children to be part of the class from outside the circle, without this being a punishment, allows the group to maintain focus on the story, while allowing a specific child to observe from a safe place.

When Joel entered the Godly Play classroom at age four he chose a space outside the circle where he could see and actually participate better because he had no fear of being "crowded," or accidentally bumped. After several months of observing from outside the circle he was able to join the circle, confident that he knew how to participate.

Over the past several years I have also discovered through reading, practice and consultation with parents, several other ideas for helping incorporate special needs children into Godly Play rooms. The issues these children faced were primarily ADD/ADHD, autism spectrum, sensory integration disorders and hearing loss. This list is not meant to be exhaustive, nor am I trying to present myself as an expert, but rather hope to invite dialogue on ways to truly invite all children into the circle.

SCHEDULE STRIP

This is a chart that can be made either for one individual, or for the entire class, with the different pieces of the class presented in order both in words and simple pictures. A Godly Play session might be broken down this way:

- story circle
- work time
- feast time
- closing circle

Each piece could be placed on its own card, which then is placed on a strip so that it could be changed to reflect the actual day. (I've seen this done very well with velcro on the back of the cards and a velcro strip.) Work days might have a card for "beginning circle" rather than "story circle" to help the child understand that there would be no story that day. You might also want a card for special events, such as Christmas pageant music practice or other events that disrupt the order of the day. The schedule strip helps children who have difficulty with focus and with transitions, because they know what's coming up so they are free to focus on what's going on right now.

PARAPROFESSIONALS

Some children might need a "para" who accompanies them during the lesson and helps them stay focused. I realize this violates the Godly Play practice of not "over-adulting" a classroom, but have found that most "paras" are excellent at blending into the background.

The bigger question, of course, is where to find people who make good para-professionals. One family in my previous parish hired their regular school para-professionals to accompany their son to large scale events such as Vacation Bible School. Older adults in your congregation may also have life experience that would enable them to be sensitive to such a job. My last two churches (in a small city) surprisingly had retired adults who had worked as special education assistants, special education teachers, older adults who had parented special needs children and occupational therapists. (It was one such retired therapist who overcame the worst of Joel's church school difficulties in addition to putting us on track for a sensory integration disorder diagnosis.).

Most children probably don't need this level of intervention on a regular basis, but if you have some that do, look around your congregation. You probably have more personnel resources than you realize!

SOCIAL STORIES

Social stories are stories about social situations that prove helpful with autistic children. There is a wealth of information about social stories online, but, basically, social stories are descriptive stories about what to expect ("my class sits in a circle to hear a story,") with some specific direction ("I sit quietly to listen to the story,") as well as some perspective on the needs of others. ("My classmates enjoy hearing the story; if I am making noise they can't hear.")

As with the schedule strip, social stories often have simple line drawings, and are read to an autistic child several times a day until they have shown a level of comfort with the situation. After that they are repeated infrequently.

MANAGING THE CIRCLE

Pay attention to space needs of individual children when building the circle. Children with sensory integration issues tend to be either very sensitive to crowding or extremely insensitive to the space needs of others. In Joel's kindergarten/first grade class there are at least two children who are hyposensitive to touch and they actively seek out sensory stimuli, sometimes without realizing it! Seating a child like Joel next to a child who seeks touch is asking for an explosion, probably from both parties.

Children who are hyposensitive might have an easier time staying focused if they have something to occupy their hands. Joel's classroom teacher sometimes gives these children beanbags filled with rice during circle time so their hands have something to do. Again, this requires awareness of how the child is doing on a given day, however, as the beanbags can be used as weapons or projectiles. I haven't noticed the other children wanting beanbags or even noticing when particular children have them.

Similarly, a child with hearing difficulty will need to be seated close to the storyteller. Being attentive to the needs of individual children takes a lot of time, but will be well worth it as the year progresses.

Children with transition difficulties might need a longer time to transition out of their work. It can sometimes be helpful to them to give them a quiet warning prior to the group warning. Alternatively, there may be some days they are so deeply engaged that they have a hard time returning to the group. Joel's teachers have been flexible about his return to the circle on those days. If children raise questions about this, you can say that he just needs a little more time today. Children are often aware of each others' special needs before adults are in classroom settings.

Be sure the circle is safe for all children, not just the special needs children. Follow the guidelines for responding to disruptions in the circle as outlined in *The Complete Guide to Godly Play: Volume 1* with as much of a combination of firmness and caring as you can muster. Help the children in the class to understand when Joel or others are having a bad day, and help them all to understand that we are all learning to work together in community. This is firm, clear teaching, not punishment.

CLOSING THOUGHTS

Talk to parents! Usually parents of children with identified needs are used to being an advocate for their child and will have many good suggestions. Parents of children who are newly identified, however, or who haven't been identified are likely to be overwhelmed or feeling inadequate. Be sure you are being supportive of them as parents, and that they don't perceive you as being another person complaining about their child or accusing them of poor parenting. Parents of special needs children have very few places they can go and feel accepted. We hope that church can be a safe place where they can find support and recharge spiritually and emotionally.

Expect that, even when doing everything we can, some days will be harder! Celebrate the good days. Look for the spark of creation that is imprinted in each child. Pray for each child and family as well as for the circle of children that makes up your Godly Play class. Pray also for yourself, that you may have a positive view of the children. Integrating special needs children into our classrooms offers a wonderful opportunity for modeling the grace of God.

CHAPTER 6
GOING DEEPER

ISABEL

When our daughters were two-and-a-half and four-and-a-half, my husband and I hired two trusted babysitters, one for Friday evening and another one for Saturday, so we could attend a local conference. Something happened that weekend with our youngest child, Isabel. Something happened that we may never completely understand. Our older daughter, Madeleine, said it was the animated movie, 101 Dalmatians, that frightened her. "I told her not to watch it," Madeleine said.

After this experience, Isabel would curl her toes and clench her fists in a posture of fear at certain times of the day. When I asked her what was wrong, she responded, "I'm scared," or "I'm afraid of the boppers." When I asked her what the boppers were, she would shake her head or maybe substitute the word "monsters." Before her father came home from work she often pleaded for Daddy. After her father came home, she would plead for Grandpa.

Of course she was unable to analyze her fears with us. She was also very quiet and fearful around strangers. Putting her to bed became torture. Isabel was truly terrified. Thus, my husband or I would sit in a chair at the foot of her bed and read until she fell asleep. I talked with our pediatrician about Isabel when the problem persisted for over a week. She concurred that it might have been something from the movie and guessed that her anxieties would continue for a few more weeks, which they did.

I offer this story as a way of thinking about children's spirituality. Although Isabel did not have words to express herself, she made herself clear with her body language and physical gestures. She "knew what she knew" and her inability to fully articulate those fears did not negate her experience. Thus, adults cannot use mere language to reassure small children. Isabel needed physical signs: holding, hugging and sitting by the bed. We did use words to comfort her and read books that echoed themes of love and safety, but words could only take us so far. Isabel's posturing suggested fearfulness and anxiety about something to which she could not put words. In short she was experiencing what might be called an existential crisis.

—by Cyndy Bishop

THE BEST WAY: GODLY PLAY AND BRAIN-COMPATIBLE LEARNING

by Becki Stewart

Godly Play is about creating a special place and time when learners, whether they are children or adults, can experience the presence of God. We are aware that the creation of this "thin place" takes much time and effort. As teachers we spend a great deal of time learning the words to the stories, organizing the environment, gathering materials and discussing the children we teach. While teaching about our Christian faith we concentrate on the content. We think deeply about the story's words and movement, how lessons fit together and build on one another. All of this is a good thing.

However, the Godly Play classroom has an invisible support system. The class structure, method of teaching, the environment and the attitude toward the learner are based upon a set of best teaching practices. Best practices form a framework that maximizes learning thus opening the door to spiritual growth and faith development.

Godly Play springs from the Montessori tradition. Marie Montessori instinctively knew what was good for children. Hundreds of examples abound—from using child-sized furniture to hands-on discovery learning. Indeed, good teachers have always found the best way to teach by "following the child." Today extensive research into how humans learn best reveals just how wise she was. The elements Montessori incorporated into her schools and learning environments match exactly the recommendations based on research done using sophisticated techniques of MRIs, brain scans, neurological science and years of educational research. This best-practice framework is an essential part of nourishing faith formation, which is the ultimate goal of our time together as Godly Players.

Although we have a deep affection for Godly Play and believe that it is the way to best help support the faith development of children, it is a helpful exercise to compare it to the best teaching practices used in education settings today. It is not enough to say, "because Jerome says so." Jerome Berryman's Godly Play exemplifies the brain-compatible model of education.

Experts in brain-compatible learning—also known now as bodybrain learning because of the direct link between the brain and all the body systems to learning—such as Eric Jensen, Spencer Kaegan, Caine and Caine, Leslie Hart and Jeanne Gibbs are some of the most notable spokespersons for this method of teaching. I'd been a Godly Play teacher for about six years when I began to learn about brain-compatible learning in the public school where I teach. Immediately I saw the parallels between this method and Godly Play. For seven or eight years, I've been working with an educational model called Integrated Thematic Instruction (ITI) authored by Susan

Kovalik. The ITI model is based on the nine bodybrain components described below. By exploring the link between the brain research on teaching and learning and Godly Play we can better implement our program with the assurance that we are teaching children the in the best way.

NURTURING REFLECTIVE THINKING: AN ABSENCE OF THREAT

The most powerful learning takes place in a trusting environment where children can explore without fear of being put down, made fun of or dismissed. Long-term learning takes place only in a safe environment where children are able to fully engage in the process. The Godly Play classroom is just such a place. Here structure and procedure provide safety. Each class follows an established pattern and activities are done a certain way. Everything from crossing the threshold to helping with the feast has a pattern. Teachers follow a format for each lesson.

Repetitive phrases such as "There was once someone…" and echoes of language that link one lesson to another provide connections that aid the learner in memory and learning. Children hear echoes of the Exodus story "they had to get up when the Pharaoh said" in the lesson about the Exile, "They had to eat what the soldiers said, go where the soldier said." The room itself is an organized and comfortable, welcoming place. Children can always find their favorite material or story. Teachers make a point to show where each lesson belongs on the shelves. This familiarity with the room helps children feel secure.

Our first duty as teachers is to create and maintain a safe environment for all children. Managing the circle from beginning to the end of the session is the storyteller's duty. He or she will guide the children through the lesson and keep the boundaries of the telling, wondering and work time. Whenever a problem arises in the circle, the storyteller assesses the situation and makes decisions that respect the individual while guarding the work being done by the community of children. Sometimes a simple redirect will work: "I need you all to be ready." On occasion the teacher must help the child choose to be ready or move to be with the door person.

The door person sits by the door to keep others from interrupting or disturbing the work of the children. When a child is not ready to be in the circle or threatens to take over the lesson, the door person is there to provide a safe place for that child to see and hear everything without disturbing others. When a child is unsure what to do with a response material or the procedure for feast, teachers assist him or her in finding the right way. The co-teachers work together showing children how to live and work together as Christians.

Perhaps the most critical element to making the Godly Play room a safe place is the respect with which the teacher treats the child. The quality of the relationship between the child and the teacher is the foundation of all that takes place here. This respect can be heard in a teacher's voice and seen in his or her body language.

Children are welcomed with a soft voice and a big smile. All children are respected, even the nontraditional learner. When a difficulty arises, whether it is a problem staying ready or interacting with another child, teachers help the child solve it without criticism. Learners are respected as individuals who have value; here even their own "wonderings" are validated.

Often the adult will respond to the child with a "hmm" or "I wonder about that, too." We too are on a journey of discovery. In Godly Play teachers don't force intimacy, but are always ready to accept hugs. Thus the open hands pose at the dismissal time. As they leave children receive an individual blessing, which reinforces that special bond between the teacher and student as well as reminding students how important they are. Every effort is made to make the child feel welcome and a valued part of the community.

The work children do in Godly Play is valued without interpretation. Teachers attempt to disappear during the work time so children's creativity is not hampered by adult presence or judgment. Their work is not "good" because we as adults say so. Rather, it's significant because it is the child's response to the lesson or deep personal needs. Children's work is not about showing they "got it" nor is it important because it pleases us. It is a gift to God.

A teacher's work also includes supporting the community of children. It is within the community that children can do their deepest reflection. We want them to slow down, focus and work through the deeply engaging existential issues all humans face. As Godly Play teachers we must be attuned to the individual child as well as the community. We constantly adjust—pause, redirect the group, extend the wondering, provide support for a child learning the story—as needed during the time we have together.

Godly Play holds dear the idea that children already have a deep spiritual connection with God. Having the opportunity to think about religious language and the existential questions all humans face is a key element of Godly Play. All children wonder about the meaning of life, freedom, aloneness and death. It is during the Godly Play time that it is possible for them to examine their own thoughts on these questions. Not only are we communicating the most sacred of our stories to children, but together we are exploring them in depth. Time spent processing the lessons through reflection builds memory of the facts, empowers the learner to make connections to other lessons and life experiences, as well as developing the capacity for introspection and listening for God. Silence is given its place in the room as we are" still and know... God."

Finally, the crucial element of reflective thinking is supported by the order of the questions used in the wondering time. These questions are carefully formulated to help the children first to enter into the creative process: "What part do you like best?" or "I wonder where you see these colors in the church?" Higher-level thinking skills are called into play when the next levels of questions are asked, "What could this really be?" or "What part is about you?"

The order of questioning is important because it invites the child to respond beginning with the easiest, most basic thinking skills. Subsequent questions then build to the more complex metacognitive skill of judgment or creativity. It should be noted that the questions are genuine and ask for deep engagement with the lesson. They are not a "test" of Bible knowledge (although that type of question has its place) or facts. Because the questions are answered with more than a "yes" or "no" the child must engage the lesson at a deeper level. They lead the child into deeper levels of understanding with the goal of deepening their relationship to God.

ENRICHED ENVIRONMENT

Children are highly sensitive to their environment. The Godly Play space is a powerful lesson in itself. By carefully constructing an environment where the learners are surrounded by the Christian language they can easily see how important the language is and how important *they* are.

Upon entering the space, the first thing one sees is the focal or altar shelf. It contains some of the most sacred images of the Christian faith—the nativity, the resurrection, the Light, the Good Shepherd. Underneath these images are the lessons for the sacraments of communion and baptism.

The choice of the materials and placement of items in the room is done with great deliberation. This place and these materials have been made especially for children. All around them they find the parables of Jesus, the sacred stories where the people encountered the mystery of God, the liturgical action lessons that show how the Christian people live together and how they worship God. Within the Godly Play room children can see a myriad of connections. A well ordered room enables children to find links between lessons, between genres, between the past, present and future, and between themselves and God. When teachers support the community of children they can create links between all the people present in the community.

A well-organized and beautiful room calls to the children. A great deal of emphasis is placed upon providing a clean, well-lit, pleasant place where the child can attain the highest state of alert awareness and enjoyment that creates deep, lifelong learning. All the materials are made for children to work with and are placed at their height. Each story or lesson is on an open shelf so a child may see and chose work. The work materials are quality materials that show value and respect for the work done in the room.

An enriched environment also provides the "real stuff," not just pictures or books about religious experience. It is a place where the experience *actually happens*. Godly Play allows the learner to engage the learning in a real, first hand way. The desert box is filled with real sand and the story is told with three-dimensional figures that move through the desert. When the lesson of Holy Baptism is presented the water, scented oil and flame are real. In the Parable of the Mustard Seed, children put the birds and nests in the tree. They actually taste the story with the *matzo* in the Exodus lesson.

The lessons provide real sensorial experiences that engage the learner's brain at the highest level. This level of engagement creates the longest lasting, most meaningful learning experience. But the materials are not the only thing that is real in the room. Here is a place where the experience really happens. We invite God to come and play. God is in the language. God is present in the room, felt by the individual and acknowledged by the community. Creating a room that is so rich in experiences makes possible a multitude of connections between the lesson, the community, God and the learner.

ADEQUATE TIME

One of the biggest challenges in our world today is "not enough time." We certainly feel that each Sunday morning. The effort to provide adequate time for the work being done in Godly Play actually begins long before the children enter the room. Dr. Berryman carefully selected a set of lessons to form the basis for his curriculum. For example, a set of "core stories" was chosen as the sacred stories. The criterion for these lessons was the encounter of the people of God with the mystery of the presence of God. Instead of making manipulatives for every single story in the Bible, he provided foundational stories that would allow children to become familiar with these essential encounters. The goal is for the learner to find their identity within the larger story of the Bible. Children who engage these stories at the deepest level develop a basic understanding that gives them greater insight into other Bible stories. Berryman spent years telling the stories—field-testing them if you will—to pare down the words, material and movements to those necessary to convey the meaning.

Also, the Godly Play curriculum is a spiral curriculum that is age-appropriate. Lessons such as the Ten Best Ways, the Faces of Easter and the parables have extensions or more materials that are presented as the children get older. Over the years as they hear the stories again, the changes in their cognitive and spiritual development mean they enter these lessons with a different set of eyes. For example, children begin with a shortened form of the Ten Best Ways when they are young. As they grow older and have an understanding of the basic lesson they learn the more complex meaning of these Best Ways.

The work of exploring questions of faith, who we are and how we belong to this community and in this language takes time. We are keenly aware that children need enough time to go deeply into the work. Adequate time encourages total immersion into the faith issues that leads to deep understanding and the ability to make meaning. The Godly Play teacher continually supports the idea of having "enough time." Throughout the Godly Play session the teacher shows having "enough time" by pausing and making space for questions and comments. For example, the wondering at the beginning of a parable is slow, encouraging children to engage in making this experience their own. Each time the lesson is told it is different. The pace and tone of the teacher's voice and movements not only respect the developing child's need to focus on where things are or the way the words go, but they remind children that this holy time is a different kind of time. People's reflection or processing time varies, so the teacher attempts to provide sufficient time for individuals create long-term learning and meaning making.

Providing adequate time requires Godly Play teachers to make choices. We can focus on one part of the session, such as the wondering, and chose to forgo another part such as the feast. Sometimes we plan work days when children go directly to their work and no lesson is given. Always in our minds as teachers is the question, "Is it time to move on or do we need to stay with the work we are doing now?" Understanding what is age-appropriate guides the teacher as she assesses the needs of the group. With older children, the wondering time often lengthens as children discuss with each other what meaning the lesson might have for them. With a younger group most often the wondering will be shorter and more to the point. They simply are not able to maintain mental concepts or attend to the lesson as long as older children

COLLABORATION

In a Godly Play classroom the community of children is the central focus. The Godly Play room offers a paradigm shift from the traditional classroom where the teacher is the dispenser of knowledge, solver of disputes, director of work and sole evaluator. To this end there are only two adults in the classroom. Every attempt is made to avoid "overadulting the room," from no private conversations between the teacher to keeping our adult eyes on the lesson. We are teaching Christian ethics about how Christian people live and work together.

Teachers provide tools for the community to work collaboratively. For example, we give children the words needed to solve problems—"Oh, you wanted to work with the desert box, too. Well, you can go ask Lindsay if you can work with her. Remember, she may say no. If she does, ask her to tell you when she is finished so you can have a turn."

During the wondering time, the storyteller acknowledges each response and shows that each child is a respected member of the group. Individual children respond to the wonderings, choose their own work and clean up their materials. Even though the storyteller presents the lesson to the community, each child comes to make the story his or her own. The community shares their discoveries during the wondering time, is ready together, has a common knowledge and purpose, and prays and shares feast together. Guidance is provided by skilled teachers who support each learner in both spoken and unspoken ways. Teachers just seem to disappear during the work time. They encourage the child who patiently waits for her turn with a smile, wink or perhaps a pat.

The community of children is also responsible for maintaining the classroom so they learn to clean up spills and sweep up the desert sand and even be storytellers to newcomers. The goal is for the learners to be totally responsible for their learning and work, as well as truly being part of the community. The work of the co-teachers is to enable them to work well individually and together.

MASTERY

Although the purpose of Godly Play is really spiritual formation, a certain level of Biblical knowledge is gained as well. In fact children who go through years of the program will perhaps be more familiar with the Exodus and the history of the Exile and return than many adults.

In Godly Play the goal is for the children to make the story their own and to be able to make meaning for themselves. Stories abound about children who find or relate the places of danger to be a certain situation in their lives or that their home is like the good, green grass. They have a strong sense that the Good Shepherd really knows their name.

Caine and Caine state in their book *Teaching and The Human Brain* that true mastery is accomplished when the learner can "use language in a complex situation and social interaction." It is evident in the conversations following the lessons that children are able to hold quite lengthy discussions about the own interpretation of the parables or how the sacred story relates to their lives.

The ability to show, explain or teach the idea or skill demonstrates a deep understanding of a concept. Besides working with art materials during the response time, children may also choose to work with a lesson. Mastery is exactly what's encouraged in Godly Play when we remind visitors or children new to the program that if they've not heard the story before "you may ask someone (another child) to tell it to you."

MEANINGFUL CONTENT

In order for real learning to take place, the learner must find the subject relevant. If the content is meaningful to the learner, he or she will be more likely to pursue a more in-depth study of it. Adults who teach children find that Godly Play is not only relevant but life changing because the lessons address the existential issues that concern all people. It is common to find people who've been teaching Godly Play for years who feel a sense of great personal attachment to it because it is so deeply meaningful. A sense of God's presence and peace experienced in the classroom can help children deal with frightening or confusing circumstances. Godly Play lessons are shared in hospitals and hospice situations as well as the typical Sunday school setting. The deep spiritual truths explored in Godly Play serve the learner whether in day-to-day living, or in times of great joy or sorrow.

The content must also be connected to and have importance for the child. The wondering question "What part is about you or where are you in the story" following the Sacred Stories encourage children to make links to their own lives. After the Liturgical lessons learners are encouraged to make connections to their own prior experiences when asked where they've "seen something like this or do they remember when…"

The Godly Play content never attempts to sugar coat the reality of the world in which we live. The wolf in the Good Shepherd parable can be the bully at school or the unknown terror that plagues our country following September 11. Noah and the Flood is not some cute fairy tale about animals two by two. Rather it requires a deep understanding and trust in the God who doesn't forget us. All of us experience the miracle of the creation in the world around us. Our own baptisms are recalled as we take our light and celebrate the light growing bigger as each new candle is lit. Liturgical action lessons help us understand our place in community and our relation-ship to the Creator. In Godly Play we are able to find a sense of identity in the sacred stories. Parables allow us to explore what the kingdom of God could really be as we hear the authentic voice of Jesus.

IMMEDIATE FEEDBACK

Immediate feedback includes the idea of intrinsic rewards for learning. For example, when a child is finally able to roll up the rug they've used for work time, they experience a sense of pride and satisfaction that sends chemicals to the brain that give a pleasurable sensation. Learning becomes its own reward. In Godly Play the children are truly working and we hope to help them achieve a "flow experience". This type of experience is described by Mihaly Csikszentmihalyi as total immersion, "a place where our heart, mind and will are simultaneously interacting and to a point where outside distractions are not able to penetrate."

The concept of immediate feedback also means correcting mistakes made by the child. For example, the control set that accompanies the Creation lesson helps children check their own work. Teachers remind children that the story is told a particular way and they help guide children as they learn the lessons. A storyteller may move close as a child works in the desert box and prompt them to follow the words or movement for that lesson. Children provide feedback to each other in the wondering time after the lesson.

CHOICES

Choice is an important brain-compatible component. Children are given many choices in Godly Play, from what material to work with, to how to respond to the lesson given or even which lesson to work with. Children may select from a variety of art materials or choose to work with a lesson they know. For the younger child a choice between chalk or crayons is the beginning. As children mature, we offer more choice in response materials: wire, wood or wax.

The open structure of the room and the availability of the lesson materials allow the child to make their own path between too hard and too easy. Choice gives children a sense of power and control. At the same time, they can choose what is most meaningful for them. This magnifies the learning. While the input or lessons are multisensory thus reaching a wide range of learners, choice in what they will make enhances the experiences for even more children. Being able to work on what is most meaningful in the medium that is your preference creates a lifelong passion for the subject.

MOVEMENT

As Maria Montessori and others have discovered the child needs movement to learn best. In the Godly Play room there is a bare minimum of furniture. Children have the space they need to move around the room to select their work, replace the lessons they used, or simply walk, look and touch things. Children may chose to clean brass objects or dust shelves. No adult lays out the work things. Instead the child goes to the shelves and gets what they need to work. The storyteller shows where each lesson belongs so that "you can get this lesson when you are ready." Children hand out the feast, make several transitions in a session and put away their own work.

The movement used in each lesson helps the child learn in a kinesthetic way. My three-year-old son was able to "show" the movement of a story he heard only once or twice even after many weeks' absence from the materials. Lessons have a core movement that identifies the story and even helps the child to make a link to other lessons. The child learns the story with his or her body long before they have the words to tell the story. Movement is key to long-term memory and understanding.

CONCLUSION

The goal of Godly Play is to teach the art of using religious language to "help children find meaning and direction in their lives while they are still young." The framework for the Godly Play class structure is a set of best teaching practices. These brain-compatible learning elements are the invisible support system we use to guide this way of faith development.

Religious language alone will not do this. We must be wise teachers who provide a way for children to enter this world of wonder and imagination so they might truly experience the presence of God. Through reflection and an open response time, children can begin to explore life's most important issues. Godly Play teaches children to live responsibly, trust their own understanding of God, and to be a part of the community of believers. Good teaching removes any stumbling blocks to faith development and opens the way for children to explore their relationship with others, themselves, nature and the Holy One.

As Godly Play teachers we continue to work on the "art of teaching." Understanding the brain-compatible learning elements and putting them into practice will enable children to find lifelong meaning in the sacred stories, liturgical action lessons and the parables. The inseparable link between what we teach (our faith language) and how we teach (brain-compatible learning) make Godly Play the best way to help children find God's direction for their lives.

CULTURAL ADAPTATION: LESSONS LEARNT SO FAR

by Rebecca Nye

Adopting Godly Play usually means people working through issues about *adapting* it for their context. Adaptation questions have been brought sharply into focus through recent work with groups in the United Kingdom, Finland and Germany who want to begin working with Godly Play, as developed in the United States of America, in rather different situations and church cultures. Although every situation is specific and has its own cultural dimension to consider, there may be general lessons too about Godly Play developing in any context. Our experiences in Europe point out two interconnecting strands to Godly Play adoption-adaptation: issues at the practical level and issues of a more psychological nature. This means that in addition to pragmatic changes to accommodate to the local conditions, there are also emotional issues that accompany undertaking Godly Play.

PSYCHOLOGICAL ISSUES

It appears there's commonly experienced resistance to wholesale adoption of all that Godly Play represents. It's wise to be aware of how natural, perhaps necessary, this response is and to understand some of the reasons behind it.

For a start, Godly Play is overwhelmingly comprehensive. It looks "too much," though that's not surprising for something that has been developing for more than three decades. However it is daunting on first acquaintance that this offers an approach to everything: using the Bible, creative activities, behavior management, learning styles, teacher spirituality, praying with children and so on. Normally, each of these would be a separate workshop or book we'd need to read. Its rare, perhaps unique, in its scope. In addition, Godly Play suggests to many people that each of these areas merits a radically different approach to what they've been used to. That's daunting, to say the least!

For some there is also suspicion that this looks "too good to be true." There can also be irritation that so much has been already carefully thought through for us. In the United Kingdom, at least, we're skeptical of "packages," especially foreign packages. "That won't work *here!*" And perhaps this reaction is quite rightly based on a practitioner's wisdom that education is a dynamic and uncontainable kind of animal.

It's perfectly natural, therefore, for imaginative teachers to feel reluctant merely to adopt Godly Play. Surely, we think, the job of the teacher is to make innovative, creative changes to what is suggested. The temptation is to treat Godly Play as a "pick-and-mix" counter of ideas. But anxieties might arise in trying to pick and mix because we're aware of the feelings I've mentioned about the daunting, even shaming, integrity and scope of the approach as a whole. You begin to wonder: is therapy necessary to get to grips with Godly Play?

Usually it's a direct experience of Godly Play that stimulates our initial interest; it seems almost impossible to describe convincingly in isolation. In fact, a sure way to create hostile resistance to Godly Play in others is probably to talk about it instead of offering it "for real!" Our own first experience of a presentation might itself be a source of emotional obstacle raising as we consider adopt or adapting Godly Play. As well as perhaps "unlearning," even undermining, many of our familiar teaching techniques, our perception of that storyteller may represent too clearly what Christian education asks of us personally and spiritually. We doubt that we could ever be that kind of storyteller—so holy, so confident, so inspired, so encouraging.

Not all of these psychological elements to taking on Godly Play have easy solutions. Perhaps it simply helps to be honest about what you feel as you try to make Godly Play work, somehow. But observing these various emotional paths and pitfalls in our work in the United Kingdom has taught us that solutions often come through foolishly, playfully "having a go" despite everything we may feel. In trying out the storyteller role, for example, despite feeling far from "holy enough," people discover that its not just the children who can feel embraced by the story and the overall structure of the session. Story and structure take the storyteller to a different, more spiritually-equipped place in themselves, too.

The teacher's need to be creative, that prompts us to wonder if we should pick and mix or even change Godly Play, in order to justify being a proper teacher, is also best solved through the experience of presenting lessons. This experience will help to reassure us that the teacher's creativity is fully needed, in a different manner than expected.

Rather than thinking up 101 ways of creatively changing the lesson in advance, or spending creative time making templates for the children to work "creatively" with (outlines to color in or paint in or make a collage with), doing Godly Play redefines creative teaching. Godly Play calls for our creativity in the lesson time itself and in our interactions with the children, in our responses to them and *their* creative work. Above all, the teacher creates a respectful space for *God*'s creative energy in the process.

Lastly, for many of the reasons above, some feel simply incapable of taking on Godly Play. Prospective teachers may like it enough to work through other emotional obstacles, yet still feel that whatever they do is never "proper" Godly Play. They may suffer from a sense that this is a rather exclusive movement that they don't deserve, or even want, to break into.

These feelings are again understandable. This approach has evoked powerful change in some people's teaching and their own faith. People's passion and loyalty about Godly Play can appear like a fence to keep out those who seem merely curious. As the criteria for developing what Godly Play teaching involves have taken thirty years so far, there's a real sense in which none of us can hope to do it "properly" for a very long time—if ever!

The good news is that with a little allowance for the emotional wobbles we and our coworkers may experience, there are plenty of ways of making Godly Play possible for your situation. Not as a lifeless perfect imitation of an impossible ideal, but as a dynamic experiment, the fruits of which you cannot predict.

PRACTICAL ADAPTATIONS

At a practical level there may be all kinds of reasons for carefully altering what the core model suggests. The scripts may be in the wrong language, or the liturgical lessons may not accurately represent your tradition. The teaching space may be shared and multi-purpose, oddly shaped or bizarrely decorated. The time available for the class may be far less than even what Jerome Berryman calls the "45-minute hour." The children may arrive hungry or thirsty, or with a need to expend some physical energy. The teachers may have different gifts, but perhaps not the confidence to learn stories easily without notes, or perhaps lack the perceptive qualities required to recognize and discuss children's spiritual work with their colleagues after the class.

Time and again people ask, "If I leave out this, or if I change that, will it still be Godly Play? Will it still *work*?" In discerning whether or not making local adaptations amounts to losing something essential—the spirit of Godly Play's well-tested vision for children's spiritual nurture—it can be helpful to learn from settings and experiences quite different from the standard. Rather than falling short of an ideal, seeing how practical obstacles have been negotiated in different places offers all of us encouragement. Successful adaptations can teach us that Godly Play is not a strict recipe for spiritual success in teaching, but an ongoing creative response to the particular situation and context we face each week.

CHANGE FOR CHANGE'S SAKE:

When people need to make changes it can help to reflect on *why* the original form exists. Because Godly Play has been evolving for so long, there's nearly always a tried and tested reason for doing things in a certain way. So if the reason for making a practical change is simply because the suggested way seems daft, consider reserving judgment. Try the original way, because chances are good that the recommendation is derived from classroom experience.

We've even managed to take a playful approach to this suggestion.

In the United Kingdom, the law requires that all children receive non-confessional, multi-faith religious education at school from ages four to sixteen. In addition schools are more generally charged to attend to the spiritual dimension of education, in all subjects and school experiences, together with the more familiar cognitive, social and moral development of children. Understandably, a matter of ongoing debate is how all these demands can be met. In a national project, directed by Alison Seaman, we've been exploring the extent to which Godly Play could inform teaching practice.

The project's school teachers in the United Kingdom were initially skeptical of giving up eye contact during storytelling. After all, the children were used to eye contact in other lessons, and group sizes were often more than thirty pupils per teacher, so there was bound to be trouble. We schemed with them that they would try storytelling without eye contact just to show what a silly idea that must surely be. They returned delighted to be proved wrong!

This "game" continued for many months as we set harder and harder tasks to test the limits of how far the traditional model could work. Surely younger classes would lose interest with lessons using flat materials? ("Can we change that?") Surely it won't work to give thirty-five children brought up on worksheets and learning aims completely free choice in response? ("Can we have a few activity areas?") Surely there's no point presenting a lesson about the Anglican church year to children who are not practicing Christians, let alone Anglicans?

Rather insisting that "this is the way it has to be done," we cheekily plotted to test it out as it was, expecting to collect real evidence of weaknesses and areas in which our situations would demand radical adaptations. Of course, you have to be able to laugh at yourself to see this through! Every time our teachers tested out something they'd have preferred to change, they returned delighted to discover something new about teaching. It had worked against their predictions and now they wouldn't change the thing they'd been so against even if we'd paid them!

Paradoxically, teachers' wisdom and experience can erode their very sense of vocation if it shuts down for them opportunities to learn and be surprised. Working with this group, as we playfully resisted making preemptive changes to Godly Play, it was clear that many vocations were refueled across all the subjects they taught. There was deep change in these teachers. However, their very different school contexts required very little changing of the Godly Play approach. In fact everyone become more and more attracted to finding ways to fit in the whole "orthodox" version.

WILL CHANGE COMPROMISE GODLY PLAY?

Of course there are many scenarios in which adapting the traditional model is necessary and where it won't be possible to even try out first hand the unadulterated version. The trick here is to at least give thought to what might be lost in choosing to proceed some other way. Take that reflection as a clue to the area in which practical compensation might be wise. Ask, "I wonder why it is recommended to do it that way, even though I really can't?" If you make a practical change, are there practical ways to attenuate the effect that could have?

For example, if a section of a script needs rewriting, or indeed, translating, it helps to remember what care and field-testing went into the given words. Every word, gesture, even every (wisely) omitted detail deserves our attention and our commitment to make refinements only in the light of how the material really works with the children.

If a change to the pattern of the session is needed—daring to leave out the feast for example—at least some of the functions of the feast might be attended to in other ways. This might mean providing some moments together before the session ends, which, like the feast, could provide the children with a clear point of return from deeply private work into the domain of the class group. This clear point of return then can offer a safe threshold back out into the collective mainstream beyond the classroom.

If you lack the opportunity to provide a specially laid out classroom, as many in older European church buildings do, it may be helpful to list what disadvantages this has. These probably include restricting the children's connections and responses to the lesson of the day, working without the safety net of the surrounding master story. Rather than simply getting depressed about this, devise ways to maximize the sense of safety, sacred space and time together to compensate. A special carpet to sit on grounds the group in more ways than we realize! Working without the unspoken lessons of a room with laid-out shelves, perhaps even more time should be spent on building the circle of the children. This can serve to recreate the coherence and security of the work space each week, and allowing time for *their* stories to fill up the room.

REAL EXAMPLES: ADOPTING GODLY PLAY IN CHALLENGING CONTEXTS

ADAPTING ENVIRONMENT

Many, probably most, English churches serve small rural communities in a single church building built between 900 and 300 years ago. There's rarely running water, bathrooms or proper heating, let alone the possibility of a separate room for children's work. And as beautiful historic centerpieces of village life, there is no chance usually of new buildings or alterations. And yet, precisely because these are typically small congregations with less than a dozen children, Godly Play could serve them very well indeed.

WoodDitton Church in Cambridgeshire is a typical example of medieval church building. The interior of the church is one continuous space—no side rooms, let alone doors for a door person to tend! But having visited a model Godly Play room, the small group responsible for children's work looked again at their situation and noticed the area under the bell tower at the back of the church. Over the years this had collected various bits of furniture stored there for no particular reason. They cleared it out and discovered a space big enough to sit in, and hung a large curtain to divide it from the rest of the church. A carpet shop gave them an remnant to lay on the floor; villagers donated redundant shelves from their homes. A kitchen unit workshop on the outskirts of the village provided some spare wood pieces onto which an artist in the congregation painted a Risen Christ, the Faces of Easter and the Days of Creation. Other materials were gradually made or bought.

Each week they have about thirty minutes with the children, during the first half of the Sunday worship service that takes place in the main body of the church space. There are, in fact, too many children to work comfortably in their new Godly Play space, so the older and younger children alternate each week over who gets to go behind the curtain! However, even when it's not "their turn," that group still does Godly Play in another corner of the church as the service continues, seemingly holding in their minds all that is provided by the carefully set out space. For all that they don't have, the implementation of Godly Play at WoodDitton has been transformative for them as well as a great inspiration for others like them.

Not having a suitable room or enough rooms for Godly Play is a common issue. Resolving to have at least *one* space for some of the children, some of the time, may be considerably better than nothing. In fact it could be a helpful way to sensitize both children and teachers to the assistance the dedicated space gives them, and the extra effort all need to expend when elsewhere.

A personal experience helped me to see how well children can carry over experience in a prepared Godly Play environment to other situations. My six-year-old daughter had enjoyed only about ten sessions in a proper Godly Play room and there had since been a break of some months. In our kitchen at home, she flicked through my copy of *The Complete Guide to Godly Play: Volume 2*, which had just arrived by post. A diagram of a Godly Play classroom caught her eye, and after a moment's study she began to describe how the diagram differed from "our room." (Yes, it does a bit!). "Our parables are over here, our art things are there," and so on. I had no idea she had internalized this unspoken structure so well, and can only wonder at how helpful that structuring of the Christian picture might have been to her on other occasions where something resonated with her unfolding awareness of religious language and story.

ADAPTING ROLES

In a set of three village churches in the United Kingdom, the really small, rather elderly, congregations made it difficult to see how to fill the roles of storyteller and door person. Sunday school in the United Kingdom usually takes place during part of the main service. Identifying both skilled storytellers and skilled door persons to run the sessions with the children seemed to point to a very tiny proportion of willing adults under the age of forty-five—the parents. As the vicar Reverend Cheryl Minor put it, to remove them from the main service every week will push the average age left in the service through the roof! The older members felt unsuited to chasing after lively children, especially on a permanent basis. They associated leading Sunday school with having to think up lessons each week, and were shy of that level of responsibility.

The solution here was realizing that, in physical terms, the storyteller role is less active than the door person's, who also might expect to respond to children's behavioral needs. Furthermore, in Godly Play, there's no need to think up lessons and activities. So a rota of more elderly storytellers has been put together, each prepared to learn a few stories and encouraged by the fact that the pattern of every class is *meant* to be the same. Godly Play does not entail a weekly, innovative concoction of educational activities to illustrate particular teaching points. Just one adult from the parents' generation acts as door person, leaving at least two others in each service.

In one school district in East London, Keith Underhill, a peripatetic storyteller and a Methodist minister, comes in to visit various classes in different schools, week by week. The local class teachers act as door persons during these sessions. This has worked out well not least because of the different vantage point it provides the class teachers on the children they teach. It also benefits the storyteller who, having put so much of himself into learning a story, has many opportunities to present and master its telling before tackling something new. He also learned about similarities and contrasts in responses to the same story from nursery children, from school children, from children at a school for special needs, as well as from adults in his usual ministry. Using Godly Play in these settings was a powerful experience of the (often) inverse relationship between a person's capacity for spiritual response and that person's capacity for intellectual and religious knowledge.

On the surface, the door person role, which is often seen as an "assistant" role, might not seem to be the obvious role for the professional teacher. However, teachers have relished the time to observe their class in a different light, to notice how absorbed in the story even the most fidgety pupils can be and to reflect on individuals without being required to respond to them immediately, such as during the time set aside for wondering. The insights provided by taking up this different position in their classroom have clearly demonstrated that the door person role requires and provides just as much professional contribution, including provision of spiritual perspective, with regard to the children as "being the teacher."

ADAPTING TIME

In contexts where Sunday school or Godly Play takes place during just part of the main service of worship, time can be very short. The question arises, what kind of Godly Play is possible in a session of only twenty to thirty minutes?

The key to adapting time in Godly Play is, I think, to remain aware of liturgical shape and its function of taking people in, with sufficient time to prepare, arrive, enjoy, explore and finally emerge from and leave sacred work. How you do that may need to vary, but leaving out one of these steps may fail entirely to model the process basic to spiritual life.

With children especially, the patterning of time associated with sacred material may leave a lifelong impression on their spiritual expectations and habits. If early experience unwittingly implies that all there is to it is "just hearing or reading the Bible, working out what it means, or being told what it means, with a bit of prayer tagged on at the beginning or end," then we may feel increasingly inadequate about our own prayer, Bible reading and theological reflection. We become aware that these activities are *supposed* to foster deeper spiritual engagement, yet when we "do" these the experience can be rather thin.

What's lacking is a spiritual protocol for making best use of time for sacred work. What's lacking is a sense of the need to get ready, to come in, to cross thresholds, to come closer, to speak, to listen and to be silent. How time is arranged with the children will help to establish personal patterns for spiritual work for years to come and in very different contexts. We have to be sensitive to the fact that merely saying to children, for example, "now it's time to pray"—perhaps just after some entirely different, potentially conflicting mental or physical activity— makes the task unnecessarily frustrating both now, and probably when they are older, too.

This is why Godly Play's traditional liturgical patterning of time makes spiritual sense at any age and for any denomination. It is about far more than simply offering children a "dummy run" of the stages of worship services, particularly the Eucharist, so that "when they go to church it'll be similar." Rather the liturgical pattern gives due attention to how, by giving time to different elements of the spiritual process, we can be helped to encounter God, respond, take leave and want to return again.

So how can this liturgical pattern, this spiritual protocol operate in a much briefer time period? In some churches in the United Kingdom, where the children have already been greeted as they entered the church, and "got ready" in the form of opening prayers with the whole congregation, that element might be curtailed in the Godly Play time. Similarly, if the children join the congregation for communion, some places have decided to omit Godly Play's feast.

In some Anglican parishes, although children may rejoin the whole congregation for communion, they may not actually receive communion themselves but a blessing instead. To trade the children's full participation in the Godly Play feast for such vicarious feasting is less than ideal, and so some congregations have elevated the significance of the coffee period after the service as an opportunity to bring the children back together informally for their special feast of juice and cookies. When surveyed, children often identify the post-worship fellowship—when we get cookies!—as one of the best things about coming to church. We adults can draw on our knowledge and experience of Godly Play to make sense of *why* this is properly significant to children's religious life!

However time affects changes that are made, it is the sense of taking time that matters most of all, rather than exactly the way that time is filled. We can remember a piece of practical advice from earlier volumes of *The Complete Guide to Godly Play*: if there's normally too little time for work, have a "work only" session every three to four sessions. If there's rarely time for a feast, from time to time devote one session entirely to having a feast. Places that have negotiated a way around very short periods with the children find that retaining the ordinary Godly Play way of beginning and ending the session is really helpful for both children and adults; there are always thresholds in and out of spiritual place and time.

We can realize that following Godly Play does not depend on "doing a story." It seems all too tempting when there are only twenty or thirty minutes available to do "just a story and a bit of wondering" *every* week. This really is not the balanced spiritual diet that Godly Play is so keen to provide as the foundation for lifelong spirituality. It's not Godly Play if there's *never* time taken over entering the space, building the circle as a community, finding ways of becoming ready, responding with individual work, sharing a feast, giving thanks and sharing the concluding blessings. Where time is short, each of these might be the extended focus *instead of the story* from time to time. Like the internalized picture of the room, this occasional attention to each part should help to provide children with relevant experience to refer to when those features of their session have to be drastically truncated.

School collective worship is another different context in which there is far from enough time to include the whole process suggested for Godly Play. In the United Kingdom all schools must provide a daily act of "mainly Christian" worship regardless of the teacher's or children's faiths. The gentle, invitational and imaginative qualities of Godly Play have greatly appealed to many teachers here. They are aware that having a moment during the busy school timetable to stop and come together as a school or group could be spiritually sustaining for both individuals and for the life of the community—if approached in an appropriately spiritual way. (Unfortunately, this has not been the favored approach. Too often "assembly" has meant storytelling with a view to moral point making, just another example of didactic teaching.)

With as little as ten minutes, schools have successfully adapted Godly Play for collective worship for assemblies ranging from thirty-five to 350 children! Some of the structure is already there; for example, the children's movement into a different space, such as the school hall, could be observed as crossing a threshold. A typical Godly Play assembly just presents a story to the children—occasionally enlarging the materials for big groups—in the same focused, intimate style as one would with a small group. The story is followed by suggesting some of the wondering questions, and offering quiet time for children and staff to reflect on these, either privately or in pairs. The opportunity to wonder aloud and to develop personal responses in other ways, such as art work, can be provided. when the children return to their classrooms in smaller groups. As an alternative, the school might provide an implicit opportunity for response by simply being a community that expects and respects people's unique voices and unique ways of "saying" throughout the school day how something has made them feel.

Ultimately adapting to or adopting Godly Play is about living out a respect for the children's spiritual life, making time and space for them and for God, and trying to be spiritually present and prepared yourself. Without those features, no amount of materials, time management to include all the "right" parts, or wondering questions will guarantee that what's going on has the value we originally experienced for ourselves in Godly Play.

ADAPTING SCRIPTS

There is now sound advice available to anyone needing to create new scripts in the process suggested for the development of object boxes. (See page 13.) As these guidelines make clear, there's a lot more to writing or adapting script than imitating the style of Godly Play presentations. In fact, well-intentioned imitations can appear to have all the right ingredients—similar looking materials, a telescoped story line, verbal and visual action and invitations to wonder—yet be light years away from authentic Godly Play, with its simple expression of truth that touches us deeply and profoundly.

When Godly Play was first introduced In Europe, some people experienced a strong need to create new material , or significantly "translate" existing Godly Play material. Some of this drive may have been due to a psychological need to make Godly Play "their own." Some of this drive may have been cultural, since educators in the United Kingdom place considerable value on teachers putting creative talents and effort into planning original lesson material for Sunday school and other contexts. Merely following extant resources can feel like cheating. Educators here also tend to be driven by theme, gathering together material, stories and activities to fit a specific theme. This tendency results in a patchwork jumble of work and work styles whose coherence is the theme, a concept which may be the least obvious aspect to the children!

In Ely diocese a theme-based children's festival at the cathedral occurred just as leaders began to learn about Godly Play. It seemed desirable to use Godly Play, but it wasn't obvious how the existing stories could be bent to accommodate the theme. It was agreed that new stories would be needed. The event, which involved more than 300 children and a team of specially inducted Godly Play style storytellers, was a clear success on many levels, and important lessons can be learnt from those attempts.

It was especially difficult to limit the amount that went into writing new scripts or new parts for existing scripts. Intellectually knowing this was a quality to aim for was not enough. Writing material really does require spiritually discerning the heart of each story, which may involve unlearning years of other Sunday school versions.

Writers were tempted too much to include the "exciting" parts of a story, at the expense of detracting from its central mood or theme. Although at one level writers were aware of children's capacity and need for spirituality, decisions about what to keep in or leave out of scripts were easily swayed by old assumptions. Stories were too influenced by what might appeal as mere entertainment, by what personal teaching points could be "put across," by how the story could fit into a general theme or by what might be considered unsuitably dark for children.

These insights of trial and error in adapting and writing scripts can be a helpful adjunct exercise to learning and using the existing presentations for some people. For example, it became clearer why it was safer to offer the children language—verbal or visual—for the dark corners, (e.g. Pharaoh's forbidding hand or Good Friday), than to make dealing with that all the children's own responsibility. Omitting the dark places inadvertently teaches that Christianity can deal only with what is lovely and transparently explicable. Changing existing stories to leave out the nasty bits, or writing new scripts that glossed over such things produced stories that lacked the capacity to hold the children and offer a safe place for their own negative experiences.

Trying to write scripts also helped some people to internalize the degree to which spiritual expression is carried non-verbally wherever possible in Godly Play. Godly Play is not just about getting the words right. Even when our mouths are shut we may be "saying too much," playing to an audience's appetite for entertainment or excitement, or inserting explanations. In fact, perhaps there is the greatest danger of becoming unintentionally manipulating and spiritually stifling within the domain of concrete, manipulative materials, as we make decisions about movements, lesson materials and imagery.

The crucial lesson learned is that Godly Play offers a well-developed language in itself. In order to say something new in it—as when we decide we need a new presentation for next week!—it helps to know already that language as fully as possible. This means there is more to writing than getting the idea of Godly Play, which would be like having a passable accent and a grasp of the grammar in a new tongue. Instead, to communicate convincingly in the language of Godly Play, it's invaluable to be familiar with its "native" phrases and customs, which often evoke a narrative in themselves. Phrases like "God came so close to Abraham, and Abraham came so close to God," or gestures of lifting and giving, are just some of the ways scripts can tell much more than an isolated story; they can hint at the integrity to be discovered in the whole.

Introducing Godly Play in non-English speaking contexts, in Finland and Germany, raises our awareness even more of issues around adapting scripts. Working with live translation is far from ideal though it may be how one begins— there is twice as much talking for a start! And speaking extra slowly to compensate, with sufficient pauses for people of any age to imaginatively enter the story for themselves, created grammatical problems for Finnish language in which the end of English sentences would normally come first.

There were many decisions to make about translating the particular sense of the words. For example, should "I wonder what you like.." take the plural or singular form of "you like"? Currently in western English-speaking settings, "wonder" is a word that has meaning at a childlike level as well as at a theological level, but it may be hard to identify such a term in other languages or contexts.

However, it was revealing how little all the problems over language really mattered. In a kindergarten setting where a storyteller spoke in English with some German translation for the children, and where occasional translation was offered to adult Finnish speakers, it was apparent that people were able to respond to the entire story which they had seen and been present to—not only what they had heard and "understood." Indeed, the experience of watching a Godly Play presentation in a language we barely know should perhaps be mandatory for adults learning this art . Such an experience would give us insight about a child's perspective on language, religious language in particular. It would help us to appreciate the "louder volume" at which small children perceive the nonverbal and the degree to which the spiritual coherence of a story is communicated through nonverbal means.

Finnish colleagues faced with the task of translation offered useful insights about the process of changing scripts. Having worked intensively for more than a week to translate the Parable of the Good Shepherd, Juha Luodeslampi experienced the story—not for the first time—as part of a class. He was struck by how utterly fresh it seemed. And yet he found translating the story, with the inevitable debates about what word to use here and what meaning was intended there, also to be deeply spiritual work. In both instances, there was considerable, but different, personal response to the material. Those of us who aren't required to wrestle with the meanings in each presentation, because they appear to be in a language we already speak fluently, might do well to admit we could be missing out.

It was also curious that Finns, unlike the British, expressed no thought of wanting to write additional new material. Their first task was to divide out the core scripts for initial translation and resolve to meet again to share critical, as well as spiritual, responses to how these stories spoke to them in their native tongue. Perhaps trying to write in Godly Play and trying to translate Godly Play are two different routes in learning to "speak" Godly Play as teachers? There may be other routes as well, but in both those cases, spending time working on the verbal and nonverbal languages used in Godly Play means working on the language for oneself, a separate activity from learning through presenting.

ADAPTING FOR CULTURE

Working in the varied contexts of the Finnish Lutheran Church, German Lutheran Church, English evangelical anglicanism, English anglo-catholicism, the British and Northern Irish Salvation Army and even some Jewish traditions in the United Kingdom naturally raises questions about the extent to which Godly Play offers something in "one size fits all."

There are obvious changes that different traditions can think about making, for example to reflect the worship environment in which the religious community as a whole worships. There's little purpose of a sacristy for a Salvationist children's room, but flags might be essential additions. Decisions about how different traditions amplify the central images of the focal shelf are also important. (Sometimes people decide to adopt something outside their tradition on the grounds that it's too helpful to the children to leave, such as marking the seasons of the church year through color.)

More subtle questions about adapting arise around theological emphasis, and often an associated tradition about the value and function of teaching. For some, Godly Play seems theologically incomplete; for example, I've been asked where the sin materials and presentations are. Others would like to give a more prominent visual position to a Bible. What is exciting about these questions and issues is how they call people to revisit their theological principles, and also their educational values. It calls us to consider our responsibilities for children's spiritual education in new ways. Does our view of faith necessitate a comparably dogmatic or liberal teaching style, or might a different teaching style, in fact, better serve the kind of faith we'd like for our children? What is *our* theology of the child? Where do we stand both intellectually and practically on the extent to which children are made in the image of God versus the extent to which they need to be molded into our image? Why do children matter to our faith? What is the Church for? What is education for? Who is God and how do we learn that?

Questions like these bubble up easily in the course of becoming acquainted with Godly Play and all that is "different" about it. This inspires creative searches for information and debates that all too often have been neglected in people's religious education. How people resolve the issues they may have with the basic Godly Play model is much less significant than the fuel this provides for taking children's spiritual foundations seriously and discerning what that means for each tradition.

GODLY PLAY IN THE QUAKER TRADITION: AN EXAMPLE OF ADAPTATION

by Caryl Menkhus

An important Godly Play material for Quakers is the Light. One of our core testimonies is, "There is that of God in every person." This core testimony is related to our peace and justice issues, to our stance against war and capital punishment and to the strong value we place on women, on children and on all people.

I often begin my year with a lesson on the Light, adapting language from the story of Holy Baptism. Instead of saying, "When you are baptized..." I talk about receiving the light when you are born. I use language they'll hear in the corporate worship, such as "holding something in the light" as an expression of our concern. This allows us to respond with what we know and value; this story and this material have a strong resonance within our own faith tradition.

I might follow that presentation with the Parable of the Good Shepherd since I want to honor another Quaker core value of listening. Each of us is wired to hear that voice; every child and every person has the capacity to hear the voice and recognize the Good Shepherd. Then I move into the stories of the People of God, followed by the Advent lessons, the parable lessons and the lessons for Lent. In our community, we recognize Lent and Advent, but "loosely," without using liturgical colors to mark the time. So I use those lessons, but without the colors. Not all Quaker communities do recognize Advent or Lent, so it's important to reflect on your community's practice and honor that.

Be very clear about how your community worships. What matters to you as a gathered community? What ways of worship matter to you that serve as openings for your community to experience God?

Be sure you understand that theologically, and choose or write lessons that fully reflect what matters if you would invite children into that community experience. Godly Play builds a bridge between the classroom and the church sanctuary. If a specific material is not something you have in your church, or that the children will experience in your church, it would be a significant question to ask yourself why you have it.

Our aim is to make God's presence more available through an examination of the symbols, gestures and silence really found in your community. Worship is not just the outward form. Silence, wonder, listening: all of these really are liturgical actions as well.

In our Godly Play classroom, there is more room on the focal shelves and more room on the liturgical shelves. We have no lessons on colors of the church year, and we don't follow the wall calendar. I intend to build a Quaker shelf, to present our story of how we as a community have learned to listen to God and come close to God. We are part of this great family who struggles to come close, finding a way to enter into the tabernacle, and looking for the way home from those places of exile we often find ourselves in.

We have lessons for the apostles and their journey. I want to continue the story by adding narratives of Quakers, such as George Fox and Margaret Fell. The testimony of their lives is a very strong message for us, and I hope that stories of this uniquely Quaker journey would wrap around part of the room extending the history of the way the people of God continue to be a part of this journey to know God. I want to include pictures of our Quaker meetings now and—a continuation of the journey—pictures of the children themselves.

What's important, and what I love about Godly Play, is that it pushes us to define, "What matters?" What is this piece of worship about that's so important that generations have captured it and handed it down? Whatever model your community follows needs to be modeled in the Godly Play classroom. What children see in the classroom must model what they would see in the whole gathered community at worship.

Every faith community has liturgy, whether they call it that or not. We can think of liturgy as a container that captures some essence of coming close to God and to one another. It matters to all of us, and all of the liturgical lessons in Godly Play help us discover and be aware of what's important to us. We can help children connect not just with the outward form, but with the inner truth of how we experience God in worship.

Now it is true that for Quakers we take a different approach to liturgy. We aren't opposed to using symbols and outward forms that help us in worship, but we really value that we can do it without those. Although symbols and outward forms mediate Christ for other traditions, our tradition says that it can be helpful but is not necessary. Communion after the manner of Friends is the experience of the reality of Christ being present among us in the silence. So I don't have lessons on my shelves to help explain the Eucharist, but I do have the Good Shepherd and World Communion. I do the whole lesson around an empty table and speak of our time of silence.

Because we don't have Eucharist in worship, we don't have a feast in the class-room. We do have prayer time. Sometimes we'll have silent prayer, and I'll end with the question, "Are all hearts clear?" That's language they'll hear in the corporate worship. We have what's known among Quakers as a programmed meeting: we have a bulletin, a prelude, a hymn, a prepared sermon, and then we have the silence. The silence lasts for 15-20 minutes, then ends with a question like, "Are all hearts clear?"

"Are all hearts clear?" Are we ready to come out of silence and listening, the vital part of worship? At the end of a lesson, I'll ask the children to be quiet for two or three minutes, to reflect on what they noticed; to consider what called to them in that lesson; to trust that God speaks to them and will lead them into what their work will be. Then I say, "Are all hearts clear? What will your work be today?"

How much silence there is in all the parts of Godly Play is a wonderful fit with our Quaker community tradition. We already have a value for the "unspoken lesson," the lesson that is communicated by our silent choices. When a community gives time and space and resources to children, the unspoken lesson is that children are valued. (Conversely, if the children's minister is told, "It's a busy Sunday; you need to be with the adults instead of the children this morning," the unspoken lesson is also clear.)

Godly Play matches the value Quakers hold for children; both traditions know that children have the same access to God as adults. Even as young children we have the ability to know God, even if that's not how we identify that experience. The simple trust that God is: we know that we know, even though we don't have the language for it.

THEOLOGICAL AND BIBLICAL PERSPECTIVES ON CHILDREN: REDISCOVERING THE VALUE OF CHILDREN AND RENEWING OUR COMMITMENT TO THEM

by Marcia Bunge

One way to enrich our interactions with children at home, at church and in a Godly Play classroom is to critically examine some of our common attitudes to children and to continually retrieve the complex view of children found within the Bible and the Christian tradition. Although all of us believe that we value children and treat them with respect, our actions often reveal otherwise. As we will see, there are six central ways of speaking about children within the Christian tradition that, when critically retrieved, serve to broaden our conception of children, strengthen our commitment to them and enrich our interactions with them.

COMMON CONCEPTIONS OF CHILDREN

Although we tend to think that we live in a "child-friendly" culture, a closer examination of our attitudes toward and conceptions of children reveals that we often view children in simplistic, narrow and even destructive ways both in the church and the wider culture. Several scholars have argued, for example, that our attitudes to children are highly informed by a consumer mentality that pervades almost all areas of our lives. Just as a market mentality has influenced our thinking about jobs and relationships with adults, it has also influenced our understanding and treatment of children. Instead of viewing all children as having inherent worth, a market mentality tends to see children as commodities, consumers or economic burdens.

The view of children as commodities is exposed most blatantly in discussions about reproductive technology and adoption. As Todd Whitmore argues, the high costs of "producing" a child through reproductive technology (anywhere from $20,000 to $50,000) reinforces the notion that a child is an "investment" from which parents can expect a "return" in the form of a "quality product."[1] The view of children as commodities or property, however, is also expressed in more subtle ways. We say that we are "having" a child and speak about how children "belong" to us. We are often tempted to view their accomplishments as extensions of our own self worth. The language of children as commodities is also seen in the discussion of parental rights. Parents say they have a "right" to raise their children as they see fit. Their children "belong" to them, and no one else has a "right" to tell them how to treat their children.

In our contemporary consumer culture, children are viewed not only as property and commodities but also as major consumers. Goods are advertised with young consumers in mind. There is almost a seamless marketing display of goods for children introduced on television, in videos and in movies and consumed in stores and fast food restaurants. Given this kind of advertising and the example of adults in their midst, it is easy for children to become highly consumer-oriented. Children pressure their parents to buy more for them and even influence their parents' purchases of items such as clothes, cars and computer equipment. The economist, Juliet B. Schor, cites studies that show most adults agree that today's youth are highly focused on buying and consuming things and that many young people themselves strongly affirm materialist values.[2]

Children are also seen as economic burdens. We see them as literally not worth our investment. They are often our last priority, and we treat them as truly the "least of these." We see this attitude toward children in the failure of many countries to care for their basic needs. For example, in the United States, 16% of children live in poverty. Approximately 9 million children have no health insurance. As Jonothan Kozol has shown, many children attend inadequate and even dangerous schools. Solid preschool programs, such as Head Start, lack full funding. We also see children as the last priority in decisions about budget cuts on the state and federal level. Road maintenance and military budgets often come before priorities to children, even though politicians pledge to "leave no child behind" in terms of health care or education. If we truly viewed children as having intrinsic value and as human beings who are to be respected and treated with dignity, then it is hard to imagine that we would neglect the basic needs of so many children in our midst.

VIEW OF CHILDREN IN THE BIBLE AND THE CHRISTIAN TRADITION

Although theologians within the Christian tradition have often expressed narrow and even destructive conceptions of children and childhood, there are six central ways of speaking about the nature of children within the Christian tradition that, when critically retrieved, can broaden our conception of children, strengthen our commitment to them and enrich our interactions with them. These six central ways of viewing children, taken together, present a much more complex picture of children than as property, consumers, or economic burdens.

GIFTS OF GOD AND SOURCES OF JOY AND PLEASURE

Christian and Jewish texts depict children as gifts of God and as sources of joy and pleasure. There are many passages in the Bible that speak of children as gifts of God and signs of God's blessing. Children are seen as ultimately coming from God and belonging to God. The Psalmist speaks of children as a "heritage" from the Lord and a "reward" (Ps 127:3). Leah, Jacob's first wife, speaks of her sixth son as a gift presented by God. (Gen 30:20). Receiving these precious gifts is also expressed as being "remembered" by God (Gen 30:22; 1 Sam 1:11,19) or being given "good fortune" (Gen 30:11). Being "fruitful" with children is being a recipient of God's blessing.

We all recognize that all children, whether biological or adopted, are in some real sense "gifts" to us. They are all greater than our own making, and they will develop in ways we cannot imagine or control. There is a mystery about conception that scientists are still exploring. Even with great advances in reproductive technology, we still do not understand and cannot control all of the factors that allow for conception and a fullterm pregnancy. There is wonder and mystery, too, in the process of adoption. Furthermore, children are more than just "our own." They are also God's gifts to the community. They will grow up to be not only sons and daughters but also husbands, wives, friends, neighbors and citizens.

Related to the notion that children are gifts and signs of God's blessing, the Bible and the tradition speak of children as sources of joy and pleasure. Abraham and Sarah rejoice at the birth of their son, Isaac. News of a son makes Hilkiah "very glad" (Jer 20:15). An angel tells Zechariah and Elizabeth that their child will bring them "joy and gladness" (Lk 1:14). Jesus speaks of a mother's joy at bringing a child into the world (Jn 16:21). Parents in the past perhaps wanted children for reasons we do not always emphasize today, such as for perpetuating the nation or ensuring that someone would take care of them in their old age. Nevertheless, there is a sense today and in the past that one of the great blessings of our interactions with children is simply the joy and pleasure we take in them.

SINFUL CREATURES AND MORAL AGENTS

By far the most common way the Christian tradition speaks of children is as sinful. Calvin states that "the whole nature" of children is a "seed of sin; thus it cannot be but hateful and abominable to God."[3] Johann Arndt claims that within children lies hidden "an evil root" of a poisonous tree and "an evil seed of the serpent"[4] Jonathan Edwards claimed that as innocent as even infants appear to be "if they are out of Christ, they are not so in God's sight, but are young vipers, and are infinitely more hateful than vipers." [5]

There are several biblical texts on which this view is based. For example, Genesis 8:21 states that every inclination of the human heart is "evil from youth." Proverbs 22:15 claims that folly is "bound up in the heart" of children." The Psalms declare that we are sinful at birth and that "the wicked go astray from the womb" (Ps 51:5; 58:3). Paul also claims that all are "under the power of sin" and that "there is no one is righteous, not even one"; all have sinned (Rom 3: 9-10; 5:12).

On the surface, this way of thinking about children can seem negative and destructive. What good does it do to speak about children, especially infants, as sinful? Isn't this view of children hopelessly out of touch with contemporary psychological conceptions of children that emphasize their potential for development and need for loving nurture? Doesn't this emphasis on sin lead automatically to the harsh and even brutal treatment of children?

Certainly, in some cases, viewing children as sinful has led to their harsh treatment and even abuse, and several recent studies have explored the religious roots of child abuse in disturbing detail. They have shown how the view of children as sinful or depraved, particularly in some strains of European and American Protestantism, has led Christians to emphasize that parents need to "break their wills" at a very early age with harsh physical punishment. This kind of emphasis on the depravity of children has led, in some cases, to the physical abuse and even death of children, including infants.

Although such cases of abuse and even mild forms of physical punishment must be rejected, and although viewing children exclusively as sinful has often warped Christian approaches to children, the notion that children are sinful is worth revisiting and critically retrieving. There are three common and helpful aspects of the notion that children are "sinful" that we must keep in mind if we are going to avoid narrow and destructive views of children.

First, when we say children are "sinful" we are saying that they are born into a "state of sin." They are born into a situation and into a world that is not what it ought to be. Their parents are not perfectly loving and just. The social institutions that will support them, such as schools and the state, are not free from corruption. The community in which they live, no matter how safe, has elements of injustice and violence. All levels of human relationships are not the way they ought to be. Another aspect of this "state of sin" is that, in addition to the brokenness of relationships and institutions in which they are born, human beings find a certain kind of brokenness even within themselves. As we grow and develop and become more conscious of our actions, we see how easy it is for us either to be self-centered or to place inordinate importance on the approval of others.

Second, when we say children are "sinful" we are also saying that they carry out "actual sins": they are moral agents who sometimes devote themselves to activities that are not life-giving but instead are self-centered and harmful to themselves and others. Speaking about a child as "sinful" is part of taking into account a child's capacity to accept some degree of responsibility for harmful actions. Within most religious traditions, including Christianity, these kinds of "actual sins" against others and even ourselves have their root in the "state of sin" and a failure to center our lives in the divine. Instead of being firmly grounded in the "infinite," in something greater than ourselves, our lives become centered around "finite" goals and achievements, such as career success, material gain, or even our appearance or approval of others. When this happens, it is easy for us to become self-centered or inordinately focused on the approval of those around us, and we lose the ability to love our neighbors as ourselves and to act justly and fairly. This view of "actual sins" of children can be easily abused when theologians equate a child's physical and emotional needs or developmental stages with sin. However, when used cautiously and with attention to psychological insights into child development, it can also strengthen our awareness of a child's growing moral capacities and levels of accountability.

Although it is important to recognize that children are born in a state of sin and are moral beings capable of actual sins against God and others, a third important aspect of the notion that children are sinful, emphasized by many theologians in the tradition, is that infants and young children are not as sinful as adults and therefore do not need as much help to love God and the neighbor. They have not gotten into bad habits or developed negative thoughts and feelings that reinforce destructive behaviors. The positive way of saying the same thing is that young people are more easily formed than adults, and it is easier to nurture them and set them on a straight path. This is one reason that most theologians who have emphasized that children are sinful have never concluded that children should be physically punished or treated inhumanely. Rather, they view them as "tender plants" that need gentle and loving guidance and care instead of harsh treatment.

DEVELOPING BEINGS IN NEED OF INSTRUCTION

A third central perspective within the tradition is that children are developing beings who need instruction and guidance. Most secular and religious traditions of childrearing assume that children are developing; they are "on their way" to becoming adults. They need nurture and guidance from adults to help them develop intellectually, morally and spiritually. They need to learn the basic skills of reading, writing and thinking critically. They also need to be taught what is right and just and to develop particular virtues and habits that enable them to behave properly, to develop friendships and to contribute to the common good.

Throughout the Bible, adults are encouraged to guide and to nurture children. They are to "train children in the right way" (Prov 22:6). They are to bring children up in the discipline and instruction of the Lord" (Eph 6:4). Parents and caring adults are to tell children about God's faithfulness (Isa 38:19) and "the glorious deeds of the Lord" (Ps 78:4b). They are to teach their children the words of the law (Deut 11:18-19; 31:12-13); to impress God's commandments on their children (Deut 6:7); and to teach them what is right, just and fair (Gen 18:19; Prov 2:9).

In our time, we might say that we are to attend to the "whole being" of the child and provide them with emotional, intellectual, moral and spiritual guidance. Thus, in addition to providing children with a good education and teaching them skills that are necessary to earn a living and raise a family, adults are to instruct children about the faith and help them develop moral sensibilities, character and virtue so that they can love God and the neighbor with justice and compassion.

MADE IN THE IMAGE OF GOD AND WORTHY OF DIGNITY AND RESPECT

A fourth important, albeit sometimes neglected, theme within the Christian tradition that helps to avoid mistreatment of children is that children are not only developing creatures but also creatures made in the image of God. If children are made in the image of God, then they are fully human and are worthy of respect and dignity. Although children are developing, they are, at the same time, whole and complete human beings. As Herbert Anderson and Susan B.W. Johnson claim, "Childhood is not merely the prelude to adulthood; the child already has the value and depth of full humanity." [6] For Anderson and Johnson, recognizing the full humanity of children is the first step toward treating all children with respect. It is also important to remember that the Bible says that God made humankind in the image of God (Gen 1:27). Thus, all children, regardless of race, gender, or class, are fully human and worthy of respect.

MORAL WITNESSES, MODELS OF FAITH, SOURCES OF REVELATION AND REPRESENTATIVES OF JESUS

In the fifth place, some passages in the New Testament depict children in striking and even radical ways as moral witnesses, models of faith for adults of entering the reign of God, sources or vehicles of revelation and representatives of Jesus. In the gospels we see Jesus touching children, healing them, embracing them, rebuking those who turn away children, and even lifting them up as models of faith. He identifies himself with children and equates welcoming a little child in his name to welcoming himself and the one who sent him. In Matthew, for example, he says: "Unless you change and become like children, you will never enter the kingdom of heaven. Whoever becomes humble like this child is the greatest in the kingdom of heaven. Whoever welcomes one such child in my name welcomes me" (Mt 18:2-5). He adds, "Let the little children come to me, and do not stop them; for it is to such as these that the kingdom of heaven belongs" (Mt 19:14).[7]

Such perspectives on children were striking in Jesus' time and continue to be striking today. At the time of Jesus, children occupied a low position in society, abandonment was not a crime and not even in Jewish literature are children put forward as models for adults.[8] Even today, we do not always emphasize what adults can learn from children.

ORPHANS, NEIGHBORS AND STRANGERS WHO NEED TO BE TREATED JUSTLY AND WITH COMPASSION

Some of the most important passages about children in the Bible have to do with our responsibility to help children in need, especially poor children. There are numerous passages in the Bible that explicitly command us to help widows and orphans—the most vulnerable in society. These and other passages show us that caring for children is part of seeking justice. They show us that love of neighbor clearly includes love of children.[9]

CONCLUSION

It is easy to dismiss the complex view of children found in the Bible and the Christian tradition and to focus on one or two perspectives of who children are. However, this has led to inadequate approaches to children today and in the past. For example, on the one hand, if we view children primarily as gifts of God and as models of faith, then we do enjoy children and learn from them. Yet we neglect to recognize a child's own moral capacities and responsibilities, and we thereby minimize the role that parents and other caring adults play in a child's moral development. We underestimate the responsibilities of both adults and children.

On the other hand, if we view children primarily as sinful and in need of instruction, then we do emphasize the role of parents and other caring adults in guiding and instructing children, and we recognize a child's own moral capacities and responsibilities. However, we neglect to learn from children, to delight in them, to be open to what God reveals to us through them. Furthermore, the role of parents or other adults thereby can be narrowly defined in terms of instruction, discipline and punishment.

We can avoid these kinds of inadequate approaches to children and can combat narrow views of children in the culture and the church by appropriating all six biblical perspectives of children. If we keep all six in mind, then we are bound to strengthen our relationships to children, to show them greater compassion, and to develop a stronger commitment to them. This commitment would include many components, but it would certainly include elements such as the following.

First, if we see children as gifts of God and sources of joy, then we will be more grateful for them and enjoy them, and we will explore the gifts that they offer to our families and communities.

Second, if we see children as sinful creatures and moral agents, then we will more readily recognize and cultivate their own growing moral capacities and responsibilities. Third, if we see children as developing beings in need of instruction, then we are bound to guide and to teach them more intentionally. Fourth, if we see children as made in the image of God and are fully human, then we will treat them with more dignity and respect—from the beginning of their lives, not just when they have become young adults. We will provide the resources they need to thrive. Fifth, if we truly believe, as Jesus did, that children can teach adults—that they can be moral witnesses, models of faith and sources of revelation, then we will be more likely to listen attentively to them and to learn from them. Sixth, if we take to heart that the Bible commands us to love and care for orphans, neighbors and strangers, and that children are also neighbors and strangers in our midst, then we will work more diligently to protect them and to renew our commitment to serving all children in need.

In these and many other ways we can combat our common misconceptions of children, enrich our interactions with them in the Godly Play classroom, and more wholeheartedly and responsibly take up the Christian call to love and care for all children.

REVERENCE FOR THE HEART OF THE CHILD

by Leander Harding

INTERPRETING CHILDHOOD

Hermes was the messenger god of ancient Greek mythology. He was depicted with winged feet as he took the message of the gods to humanity. When a message is delivered there is always the problem of understanding, of interpretation. You need some principles of interpretation that help you understand what you are hearing and what you are seeing.

When scholars want to study principles of interpretation or develop a theory of interpretation, it is called the study of hermeneutics. In what follows I want to call attention to the fact that each one of us has a hermeneutics of childhood. We have some principles of interpretation, some presuppositions about human nature and the nature of childhood that we bring to our interaction with our children, and which we use to make sense of what we hear and what we see. There are some ways of seeing children that encourage respect for the child, and some which make it very hard to have such respect.

HOW DO WE SEE CHILDREN?

Each of us has a way of seeing the world that is based on our understanding of how the human heart works, and which acts as a set of spectacles. As we look at our children through this set of spectacles we see them in a particular light. If you have ever had your eyes examined you know the experience of having the doctor let you try different lenses. Some lenses make things blurry, some cause things to come into focus, and you can finally make sense out of the eye chart. The doctor even explained to me that a lens can cause you to see things more clearly than they really are. If you wear glasses you have also had the experience of forgetting that you are wearing them.

If we are to do justice to our children, we need to be aware of the lenses through which we are seeing them and ask if these spectacles allow us to see our children fully and clearly.

An example may help. I used to drop my oldest son at Kindergarten. The school was very firm about not allowing anyone to enter the building before a particular time.

The parents and the children would line up outside the door and wait for the bell to ring. As they waited for school to start, the parents would talk.

One day I overheard one mother speaking to another about the difficult night she had just had with her new infant. "He cried and cried," she said. "finally I just shut the door on him and let him cry it out."

Another mother replied, "Yes, that is right. It is a battle of wills and you can't let them get the better of you. You can't let the baby manipulate you."

I was very sympathetic to the struggle of the tired mother with a crying infant. Both my wife and I have walked miles holding crying infants. But I was struck by the power of interpretation that was at work in this exchange. I was struck by the hermeneutic, the way of seeing childhood, that was being shared between these two mothers.

The cry of the child was being interpreted as part of an ongoing, even desperate, struggle between the will of the parent and the will of the child to see who will dominate. All we know for sure is that a child is crying in the night. The advice to listen to a strong maternal instinct and pick up the child and hold it all night long if need be, or the advice to close the door and let the child cry it out, will depend on how the cry is interpreted. We know for sure that the child is crying in the night. It could be just as serious as it sounds.

To see the child as essentially greedy, selfish and willful is a particular hermeneutic of childhood that has its roots in some strands of the Christian Tradition. There are great Christian teachers who have stressed the reality of sin and the fallenness of human nature. Other teachers have stressed the essential goodness of human nature made in the image of God.

Both the goodness of human nature made in the image of God and the reality of sin need to be kept in balance in a Christian understanding of human nature. We are inherently capable of goodness, creativity and love. We also turn away from God and from each other and are capable of evil.

If our hermeneutic, our way of seeing children, sees the child in either too negative a light or too positive a light we are likely not to be able to see things about our children that are very important. We are likely to misinterpret their behavior and respond to them in ways that are based on misunderstanding, rather than deep understanding.

Our children are neither worse nor better than we are. They are made good in the image of God and are tempted by evil just as we are. They are neither little angels nor little demons. They are human beings just like their parents. To see them as being worse than they really are, or more noble than they really are, can hurt them and do them an injustice.

Each one of us has deep need to be seen, accepted and loved as we really are. If we are never seen to be good or even capable of good, this hurts. And if we are seen to be so good that goodness is not a struggle for us, this hurts as well.

Our faith presents us with a very realistic understanding of human nature, and it can help us understand the reality of our children. Our children's sense that we truly understand them and sympathize with them is one of the things that builds trust and love, and which motivates them to try to do those things which we value and honor.

In the world of psychology there has been the same tension between seeing children, as either naturally good or naturally selfish, that we have seen in the history of religious thought. Sigmund Freud, the great Viennese doctor and founder of modern psychology, thought of children as little savages governed by overpowering physical instincts for the satisfaction of natural appetites, including the appetite for sex.

Parents and society needed to restrain and discipline the needs of the libido so that children could become functioning members of society. In a way the Freudian hermeneutic of childhood is a kind of secular version of what some theological writers called the "utter depravity of human nature."

A RELATIONAL VIEW OF CHILDREN

Since World War II some psychologists and psychoanalysts have developed another way of seeing children—a way that they feel is more consistent with the reality of the children that they are seeing in their consulting rooms. This school of thought is referred to as Object Relations Theory. These writers see that children do indeed have many instincts and desires like all human beings, but they believe that the strongest need that children have is for relationship. If this is need is frustrated, children can become emotionally and physically sick—and I would add that their ability to develop and grow in faith may be adversely affected.

Alice Miller is a Swiss psychoanalyst who has written extensively about childhood from this Object Relations perspective. Miller says that the primary need children have is the need to be loved. Love is different from admiration. Love is nurturing. Admiration is toxic. Love is unconditional, while admiration is conditional. A child needs to see that his or her parents, especially the mother, sees who he or she is and accepts, values, loves the child for who he or she is.

The child needs to look into the face of the parents, and especially as an infant, into the face the mother and find him or herself in the returning gaze of the parents. The child needs to have his or her reality acknowledged and validated by the parent. This does not mean that we approve of everything we see in our children, but it does mean that they see that we see them, and they we acknowledge that their feelings are real and valid.

Love is the ability to give to another human being, and especially to our children, this accepting, valuing attention. No one is able to do this perfectly. It is easy to give our children our attentive regard when they are showing us something pleasant and agreeable. If the child is interested in us—loving, pleased and pleasing—it is not hard to focus our loving attention on the child. When our children show us something that is upsetting or disturbing, it is human to tend to withdraw.

When you are an infant and your care givers withdraw their attention, it feels life threatening. You will do anything to keep that gaze upon you. Children have a kind of radar about what makes their parents emotionally comfortable, and what makes their parents uncomfortable or anxious. If too much anger, too much enthusiasm, too much delight in their own bodies causes the parents to become anxious and emotionally withdraw, the child will try to hide those parts of him or herself.

When you are an infant and a small child you live in a glass house and the only place to hide things is underground. These parts of the child's personality become cut off and buried. As an older child or adult, the person forgets where these parts of their personality are buried. Children begin to develop a false and conforming self, while important aspects of their real self remain cut off and buried.

A CHILD'S RAGE

One of the parts of the true self that often gets buried is the rage and anger that the child feels at having the deep human need for relationship frustrated. The child needed to be seen and acknowledged, honored and validated, and this need has been violated. This is an experience of outrage, and this feeling of outrage is so threatening that the child cannot risk showing this to the parent.

The only way not to show it is not to feel it, to cut off and bury this feeling. These cut off feelings and aspects of the true self turn poisonous, and this repressed rage often gets projected inward as depression and self-destructive behavior, or outward as hatred and violence toward others.

ADMIRATION OF CHILDREN

All children end up burying some parts of their true selves. Most children have what has been called "good enough" parenting. Their parents can love and accept them well enough so that they are able to come out of childhood with enough of a solid self to grow and develop as healthy adults.

Sometimes children have not enough love in their lives and too much admiration. According to Alice Miller, admiration is attention given on a conditional basis. I will attend to you and maintain my connection to you as long as you show me things that make me feel good—that comfort me, that reduce my anxiety. The sub text of the message of admiration is always. "I love you now, but my love may be withdrawn at any moment you show me something that makes me uncomfortable."

In such a circumstance the normal balance of the relationship is turned upside down. The child exists for the sake of the parent, and the focus shifts from the emotional needs of the child to emotional needs of the parent. Children in such circumstances really lose themselves and often become good, dutiful but joyless adults.

One of the characteristics of admiration is that it takes more and more admiration to provide less and less emotional satisfaction. Children who are admired, rather than loved, are desperate for attention. Often they are not able to get the kind of loving attention they really need.

It is part of the sadness of this pattern that a deficit of human love can make it hard for these children to feel and believe in God. These are the children who are easily led astray by peer pressure, and become prime targets for cults. They are easily bought by displays of attention, and really do not know what they think or feel.

The way we think about childhood, and the way we see children, can make it easier to see our children and their needs, and to offer them love. Or the way we see children can make us prone to offer a conditional admiration.

THE CHILD'S NEED FOR THE LOVE OF GOD

Understanding this dynamic of childhood helps us see the importance of the experience of the love of God for normal human development, and helps us understand why an approach like Godly Play is especially appropriate to the emotional development and spiritual needs of children.

In order to develop a true self which is capable of a growing intimacy with other people and with God, children need to experience love rather than admiration. There is no earthly parent who is able to give pure love. It is inevitable that our love for our children will be mixed with admiration.

In our relationship with our children, we cannot always keep them at the center of our attention in the way that they need, and at the time that they need. Children have a need for love that is beyond the capacity of even the most attentive and loving parents and teachers to provide. Children have a need for the complete and perfect love of God—whose gaze is unfailing, who sees all and never withdraws, who accepts everything about us, both good and bad, and loves us anyway; and who offers us strength and help in the struggle with evil and the struggle to love as we are loved.

At first this love needs to be mediated to children by their parents who, to the best of their ability with God's help, love their children as they themselves are loved by God, out of all proportion to any desert or merit.

THE LOVE OF GOD FOR THE CHILD MEDIATED THROUGH GODLY PLAY

Ultimately this love which is mediated in the relationship between the parents, teachers and children needs to be available to children in a more direct way. The religious materials of Godly Play give children an opportunity to become engaged in a very direct way with the experience of the Love of God. As Sofia Cavaletti says, this way of working with the religious education of children allows the cry of the child, "let me experience God for myself," to be answered.

As the children interact with the materials in an atmosphere that is permeated with a philosophy of respect for the child, the children are able to experience the deep love which they need in order to find and develop their true selves, and to grow emotionally and spiritually strong. As they manipulate the materials they are able to engage parts of their experience which have been cut off and buried, and to reexperience these elements in the face of the total acceptance and love of God. They are able to acknowledge and engage their temptations and the reality of evil, and to find that God is really their helper.

In touch with the love of God, these children will not be easily manipulated by the need for admiration. They will know who they are and what they think and feel, and what is true and good and beautiful. They know God loves them just as they are, forgives them when they are wrong and helps them to be better. By giving our children Godly Play we give them an experience of the love of God that fills their deepest needs, and which will make it possible for them, in their turn, to put their children in touch with the never failing source of love.

OUR NEED FOR GOD'S LOVE

All that I have said here about the need that children have for an encounter with the love of God holds true for each one of us as well. Our ability to offer our children a nurturing love, as opposed to a poisonous admiration, will depend on our experience of being loved. We need to have the love of God mediated for us by other people. We need that direct contact that comes from an immersion in religious symbols, in the words of the scripture and in the sacraments of the church.

As parents, teachers and caretakers of the young, we need the conviction that God sees the secrets of our hearts, and does not draw back; sees how hard it is for us to be as good as we want to be and comes to help. Knowing this will help us look upon our children with love, and will help us be genuinely helpful to their desire to honor God.

ENDNOTES

1 Todd David Whitmore with Tobias Winright, "Children: An Undeveloped Theme in Catholic Teaching," in *The Challenge of Global Stewardship,* edited by Maura A. Ryan and Todd David Whitmore (Notre Dame: University of Notre Dame Press, 1997), 171-172.

2 Juliet B. Schor, *The Overspent American: Why We Want What We Don't Need* (New York: Basic Books, 1998), 87.

3 John Calvin, *Institutes of the Christian Religion: 1536 Edition,* translated by Ford Lewis Battles (Grand Rapids, MI: Eerdmans, 1975), 97. Quoted by Barbara Pitkin, "'The Heritage of the Lord': Children In the Theology of John Calvin," in *The Child In Christian Thought,* edited by Marcia Bunge (Grand Rapids, MI: Eerdmans, 2001), 167.

4 Johann Arndt, *True Christianity*, trans. Peter Erb (New York: Paulist Press, 1979), 34-35.

5 Jonathan Edwards, *Some Thoughts Concerning the Present Revival* (1742), in *The Great Awakening*, edited by C.C. Goen (New Haven: Yale University Press, 1972), 394. Quoted by Katherine Brekus, "Children of Wrath, Children of Grace: Jonathan Edwards and the Puritan Culture of Child Rearing," in *The Child In Christian Thought,* 303.

6 Herbert Anderson and Susan B. W. Johnson, *Regarding Children: A New Respect for Childhood and Families* (Louisville, KY: Westminster/John Knox Press, 1994); 9.

7 Some of the most significant passages in the gospels are Mark 9:33-37, Luke 9:46-48, Matthew 18:1-5; Mark 10:13-16, Matthew 19:13-15, Luke 18:15-17; Matthew 11:25 and 21:14-16. For a discussion of views of children in the gospels and in the New Testament as a whole, see Judith Gundry-Volf, "The Least and the Greatest: Children in the New Testament," in *The Child in Christian Thought,* 29-60.

8 Gundry-Volf, "The Least and the Greatest: Children in the New Testament," 39.

9 See, for example, Ex 22:22-24; Deut 10:17-18; 14, 28-29.

OTHER TITLES AND VIDEOS IN THIS SERIES

THE COMPLETE GUIDE TO GODLY PLAY
BY JEROME W. BERRYMAN

An imaginative method for presenting scripture stories to children

This five-volume series invites preschool through 6th-grade children to discover God, themselves and one another through our sacred stories. Based on Jerome Berryman's work in the Montessori tradition, *Godly Play* uses a careful telling of scripture stories, engaging story figures and activities to encourage children to seek and find answers to their faith questions. *Godly Play* respects the innate spirituality of children and encourages curiosity and imagination in experiencing the mystery and joy of God.

HERE'S WHAT YOU GET IN EACH VOLUME:

• **VOLUME 1: How to Lead** *Godly Play* **Lessons** contains all of the material you will need to be familiar with the *Godly Play* approach, including how to create a special space for children, plan and present the lesson and help children develop spiritually. 1-889108-95-2

• **VOLUME 2: Fall** - an opening lesson on the church year followed by 13 Old Testament stories, from Creation through the prophets. 1-889108-96-0

• **VOLUME 3: Winter** - includes 20 presentations based on stories about Advent and the feasts of Christmas & Epiphany, followed by the parables. 1-889108-97-9

• **VOLUME 4: Spring** - presents 20 lessons covering stories of Lent, the resurrection, the eucharist and the early Church during Easter Season. 1-889108-98-7

• **VOLUME 5: Practical Helps from Godly Play Trainers** - experienced trainers and teachers share insights, stories and ideas for using *Godly Play* to its fullest. 1-931960-04-6

HOW-TO VIDEOS NEW

Masterful *Godly Play* storyteller Jerome W. Berryman guides catechists through two actual *Godly Play* sessions per season. In this three-part series, listeners are enthusiastically engaged in how to tell the story and invite children to experience the wondering.

Available in VHS & DVD formats

To purchase these products, contact your local bookstore or call Living the Good News at 1-800-824-1813.

www.livingthegoodnews.com

THE COMPLETE GUIDE TO GODLY PLAY
VOLUMES 1-5   **$ 24.95 each**

Sessions are adaptable from 45 minutes to 2 hours and include a complete materials list. 8 1/4" x 10 3/4", 120 pages, paperback

FALL VHS OR DVD	**$ 24.95 each**
WINTER VHS OR DVD	**$ 24.95 each**
SPRING VHS OR DVD	**$ 24.95 each**

Approximately 45 min. each.